The Pith of the Apocalypse

The Pith of the Apocalypse

Essential Message and Principles for Interpretation

Paul A. Rainbow

WIPF & STOCK · Eugene, Oregon

THE PITH OF THE APOCALYPSE
Essential Message and Principles for Interpretation

Copyright © 2008 Paul A. Rainbow. All rights reserved. Except for brief quotations in critical publications or reviews, no part of this book may be reproduced in any manner without prior written permission from the publisher. Write: Permissions, Wipf and Stock Publishers, 199 W. 8th Ave., Suite 3, Eugene, OR 97401.

Wipf & Stock
A Division of Wipf and Stock Publishers
199 W. 8th Ave., Suite 3
Eugene, OR 97401

ISBN 13: 978-1-55635-914-9

www.wipfandstock.com

Manufactured in the U.S.A.

Unless otherwise indicated, biblical quotations are from the Revised Standard Version of the Bible, copyright 1952 [2nd edition, 1971] by the Division of Christian Education of the National Council of the Churches of Christ in the United States of America. Used by permission. All rights reserved.

Contents

Preface vii
Acknowledgments ix
Note on Abbreviations xi

1 Invitation to the Revelation 1

2 Situation of the Recipients 13

3 Literary Structure 28

4 Cracking the Code 45

5 Main Theological Concepts 67

6 Eschatology 85

7 Preaching and Teaching It 111

Bibliography 123
Scripture Index 139
Subject Index 159

Preface

At the urging of ministerial students and lay parishioners who have explored the book of Revelation in my classes I offer this slim volume to the public. My students come from a wide swath of backgrounds representing mainline Protestants and fundamentalists. The more enlightened have little idea what to make of the Apocalypse. Some others think they already know exactly what it means, and which expositors alone are trustworthy.

My aim is to open up the book to the bewildered by explaining some generally accepted principles of interpretation that any thoughtful person can use to penetrate its message. The present study is intended for practicing clergy and theological students; for questing lay leaders who want an approach informed by recent scholarship; even, in places, for scholars prying into unsolved problems (see esp. Chapter Three, on the literary structure; and the end of Chapter Six, on the millennium).

I have set myself the task of being both intelligible and concise. It would be impossible in a short space to argue an academically rigorous case for each position taken, against every alternative in a field as rife with hypotheses as is the case with the Apocalypse. A positive basis in the text of the book for each assertion must suffice. My general approach has been molded by dialogue with critical study within the great tradition of Christian orthodoxy and should commend itself as worthy of consideration in diverse Christian circles.

The path I pursue is Preterite Idealism. I recognize, with most critics, that John wrote primarily for his own day and addressed issues he and his churches faced (preterism). With the orthodox tradition, I hold that the apocalyptic element was no mere husk, only partially fulfilled in its time, that can now be stripped off from the moral and spiritual kernel of John's message by demythologization, but contains truths that were not exhausted in the events that transpired toward the end of the first century, that remain perennially valid until their grand fulfillment at the end of time, and speak to believers of every epoch with promises of judgment and of salvation (idealism). It is my prayer that anyone who works through the chapters of the present volume will be incited to respond in faith and obedience to the challenge of the Revelation in its elemental power and beauty.

Acknowledgments

Acknowledgments are due to the Administration and Faculty and the Board of Trustees of Sioux Falls Seminary for approving a semester sabbatical in autumn 2005, during which I wrote; to Linda Watts in the Kaiser-Ramaker Library for her assistance in obtaining materials by inter library loan; and to my wife Alison for all she is and does.

Note on Abbreviations

Abbreviations in this work to scholarly publications follow the standard lists in *The SBL Handbook of Style* (ed. Patrick H. Alexander, et al.; Peabody, Massachusetts: Hendrickson, 1999).

I

Invitation to the Revelation

WRAPPED IN some of the most graphic imagery of the Bible, the book of Revelation conveys a vital message of warning and encouragement. It takes us behind the stage of earthly temptations and troubles to disclose the divine Majesty whose plan for the ages is unfolding inexorably toward the goal he has pre-ordained, and lets us see the total victory Jesus has already staked out over our direst foes, even over death itself. It sternly admonishes Christians not to participate in the hubris of society, while holding out promises of extravagant rewards for humble followers of the Lamb who find themselves forced along the way to pay the price of social ostracization or martyrdom.

Bracing though this message is, it is neglected by many potential readers. The forte of the writing, its vivid picture language that strikes viscerally and memorably, makes it a playground for eager interpreters. While most attempts to explain the Apocalypse have been sincere, their results have scarcely been in agreement. Put off by strident views and equally dogmatic counters on the part of reputed experts on biblical prophecy, large numbers in the pews turn away from the Revelation in perplexity or outright distaste. Others, less savvy, get drawn into one school of interpretation (such as dispensationalism, the theological system behind countless radio sermons, the bestselling *The Late Great Planet Earth*[1] and the Left Behind Series

1. Lindsey, *Late Great Planet*.

novels[2]), perhaps unaware that options for interpretation exist that are arguably more faithful to the original intent.[3]

Nevertheless the gist of this enigmatic book can be understood, and it is rapidly coming to light in the main stream of recent scholarship on the New Testament. During the course of the twentieth century, biblical specialists came to share a common set of interpretive methods, and made signal advances in exploring the Bible against the backdrop of the ancient Near Eastern, Jewish, and Greco-Roman environments in which its constituent books were written. Not every riddle in the Apocalypse is solved. But by making some reasonable assumptions at the outset we can clarify the main lines along which a responsible interpretation of the Revelation must move.

ASSUMPTIONS

A sound framework for understanding the Apocalypse begins with the following assumptions, gleaned from the book itself, especially from the superscription (1:1–3).

> *1. The book of Revelation belongs to the category of inspired scripture and deserves to be read by the church as part of the canon of sacred scripture.*

In the first sentence the author tells us he received the matter from God by the agency of an angel, making it "the word of

---

2. Beginning with LaHaye and Jenkins, *Left Behind*. Sociological study of the impact of the series: Frykholm, *Rapture Culture*. Alternatives to the kind of interpretation undergirding the Left Behind series: Rossing, *Rapture Exposed*; Koester, "Revelation and *Left Behind*."

3. For an exposition of dispensationalism, see Ryrie, *Dispensationalism*. Dispensationalist eschatology was systematized in Pentecost, *Things to Come*. A leading commentary from this perspective: Walvoord, *Revelation*. Critiques: Bass, *Backgrounds to Dispensationalism*; Gerstner, *Wrongly Dividing the Word*.

God" and "the testimony of Jesus Christ" (1:1–2), motifs that crop up again toward the end (19:10; 22:16, 20). While he was "in the Spirit" (1:10), he heard oracles of the risen Christ (2:1, 8, 12, 18; 3:1, 7, 14), each spoken by the Spirit (2:7, 11, 17, 29; 3:6, 13, 22). Later came an invitation to ascend into heaven and view things about to transpire on earth, at which immediately he was "in the Spirit" again (4:1–2; cf. 17:3; 21:10).[4] Throughout the book the author reports frequent interactions with angels (6:1–8; 7:13–14; chap. 10; 11:1–2; 17:1–3, 7–18; 19:9–11; 21:9–10, 15, 22:1, 6, 8–11). Again and again he is told to write down what he is hearing and seeing (1:11, 19; 2:1, 8, 12, 18; 3:1, 7, 14; 14:13; 19:9; 21:5; contrast 10:4). In summary statements the words of the prophecy are declared faithful and true (19:9; 21:5; 22:6). At the end stands a threat not to tamper with the text (22:18–19). How could the author have laid stronger claim to divine inspiration?

Merely to lodge a claim is not, of course, to establish it. Other apocalyptic writings of the same era were not canonized. But already within the next generation, copies of John's Apocalypse were being circulated and studied in Asia Minor (modern Turkey) among some who had known the author there face to face.[5] Justin Martyr, among the earliest ecclesiastical authors, referred to it.[6] Within a century or so after publication it was being cited in places as widely distributed geographically as Gaul (modern France),[7] Rome,[8] western Syria,[9] and Alexandria

4. Filho, "Apocalypse as a Visionary Experience."

5. Irenaeus, *Against Heresies* 5.30.1 (*ANF* 1:558).

6. Justin, *Dialogue with Trypho* 81 [c. A.D. 161–165] (*ANF* 1:240).

7. Letter of the churches of Gaul to those of Asia and Phrygia, in Eusebius, *Ecclesiastical History* 5.1.10; 5.1.58.

8. Muratorian Canon. Hennecke, *NT Apocrypha*, 1.45, line 71.

9. Theophilus of Antioch, *Against Hermogenes*, cited in Eusebius, *Eccl.*

in Egypt.[10] While its abuse by Montanists and other millennarian sects looking for an earthly vanity fair led some individual church leaders to react against it,[11] by the end of the fourth century most doubts had been dispelled.[12] For the last sixteen centuries the book of Revelation has held an honored place in the canon of New Testament scriptures accepted by Roman Catholics, the Eastern Orthodox, and Protestants alike.[13]

It pronounces seven blessings upon those who read and keep what it says (1:3; 14:13; 16:15; 19:9; 20:6; 22:7, 14).[14]

2. The Apocalypse was designed to communicate, not to obfuscate.

For many Christians, to read the book of Revelation is to enter a bizarre world. What are the plethora of images meant to denote? But by superscribing the work an "apocalypse"—according to some translations, a "revelation"(1:1)—the author indicated his intent to make his burden plain rather than obscure. The noun *apokalypsis* is a compound of two Greek roots, *apo* "away," and *kalyp-* "to cover." It points to the process (*-sis*) of taking the cover off something, an unveiling.

Further along in the opening verse, two verbs indicate what kind of communication the book contains. "To show" (δεῖξαι, *deixai*) is to point to a visible object. "To make known" (σημᾶναι, *sēmanai*) is to use a sign. Both verbs state what is ob-

---

Hist. 4.24.

10. Clement of Alexandria, *Paedagogus* 2.11 (*ANF* 2:265); *Stromata* 6.13 (*ANF* 2:504), 6.16 (*ANF* 2:513).

11. E.g., Gaius of Rome; Dionysius of Alexandria; see Eusebius, *Eccl. Hist.* 3.28.1–5; 7.24–25.

12. Athanasius, *Easter Letter* 39.5 [A.D. 367] (*NPNF*² 4:551–52).

13. De Groote, "Kanonbildung im Westen"; "Johannesapokalypse und Kanonbildung im Osten."

14. Nwachukwu, *Beyond Vengeance*.

Invitation to the Revelation 5

vious in any case, that the work makes generous use of symbolic language. It does so in the interest of letting the reader see.

Yet if John wished to make himself clear, why adopt such an esoteric mode of speech? John and his implied readers stood in a literary tradition rooted in the Hebrew scriptures. Israel's historical saga, legislation, poetry, and prophecies, driven deep by a Jewish rearing so as to become the presuppositional grid through which John construed reality, formed the stockpile of known material upon which the divine Spirit played to awaken in his mind glimmers of the unknown future. There is no dilemma whatsoever between John's claim to have experienced fresh visions, and the fact that his record of those visions is a tissue of allusions ranging over the whole of the Old Testament. The dense language of the Revelation will cease to be an obstacle to modern Christians, to the extent that we too familiarize ourselves with that literary heritage, especially key parts of Isaiah, Ezekiel, Daniel, and Zechariah.[15] When John's symbols evoke past associations in the new patterns into which he presses them, his writing gains a luminosity and a punch it could never have packed had he written in a vacuum.

3. *The book of Revelation is a book of prophecy in the tradition of the Hebrew prophets.*

John designates his writing a "prophecy" (1:3; 22:7, 10, 18, 19), and his own activity of delivering it, "prophesying" (10:11). Yet what establishes its contribution to the prophetic literature of the Bible is not so much these explicit self-descriptions, as

15. On John's use of various parts of the Old Testament in the Revelation, see Beale, *OT in Revelation*; Pisano, *Radice e stirpe*; Fekkes, *Isaiah and Prophetic Traditions*; Kowalski, *Rezeption des Ezechiels*; Sänger, *Ezechielbuch in Johannesoffenbarung*; Jauhiainen, *Zechariah in Revelation*; Dumbrell, *End of the Beginning*; Mathewson, *New Heaven and New Earth*.

the degree to which the entire opus takes over and reworks language, imagery, issues and conceptions from the oracles of the Old Testament. Indeed, the book gives the impression of a deliberate summation of the entire sweep of biblical prophecy (note esp. 10:5–7).[16]

Scholars have bled plenty of ink on whether the Revelation is more appropriately classified as prophetic or apocalyptic literature. Prophecy, the goal of which was to call an unfaithful people back to the terms of God's covenant, at first oral and then written, makes up a sizable portion of the Old Testament, from Isaiah to Malachi. Apocalyptic was a literary type that flourished later, among erudite Palestinian Jews during three centuries of hardship between the Seleucid king Antiochus Epiphanes IV (mid 160s B.C.) and the crushing defeat under the Roman emperor Hadrian (A.D. 135). Taking their cue from Daniel, these Jewish mystics enjoyed tours of heaven or received visions of things to come and wrote their secrets down. Their literary productions influenced one another in succession. They share motifs such as an expectation that the end was near, charts of future events, the rise of a world regime that would persecute the saints, the arrival of the messiah to scatter their enemies, and the dramatic descent of God as judge and benefactor.[17]

Prophecy and apocalyptic have sometimes been contrasted in broad strokes, the former viewing God as immanent in the historical process to bring about his kingdom, the latter depicting him as having given a corrupt world its last chance to repent and being ready to intervene from above. Historically, however,

---

16. Bauckham, *Theology of Revelation*, 5, 117, 144. Note also the title of a collection of the same author's essays: *Climax of Prophecy*. See also Kyrtatas, "Apocalypse"; Heike and Nicklas, *Worte der Prophetie*.

17. On Jewish apocalyptic literature, see Rowley, *Relevance of Apocalyptic*; Rowland, *Open Heaven*; VanderKam and Adler, *Jewish Apocalyptic Heritage*.

Jewish apocalypticism developed from select passages of Israelite prophecy, and the apocalyptists saw themselves as standing in direct continuity with the earlier prophets.[18] The distinction between prophecy and apocalyptic was an illusion created by certain modern attempts to impose a taxonomy on ancient material. John's Revelation is a prophecy that has absorbed apocalyptic trademarks from some of its younger forebears.[19]

Determining that the Revelation is a prophecy helps us know better what to expect from it. Biblical prophecy is always a summons to persist in listening to God and doing his will, in view of the absolutely certain ripening of God's good purpose, even if a surrounding civilization has chosen a course leading to divine judgment. Any interest in the secrets of heaven above or in the future is not merely for the sake of knowing things outside our ken, but to ensure that God's people are readying themselves for theophany. It is for those who "keep" the things written in the prophecy that a blessing is promised, from beginning (1:3) to end (22:7).

4. The Apocalypse is a genuine piece of communication between a first-century author and first-century readers.

Our author identifies himself as "John" (1:1, 4, 9; 22:8). Critics who doubt whether he was the apostle nevertheless accept the name. Patristic writers as early as the second generation after his death knew of a firm and widespread oral tradition stemming from Asia Minor that he was the apostle,[20] who had migrated to Ephesus and settled there when Jewish refugees fled

18. Hanson, *Dawn of Apocalyptic.*

19. On the apocalyptic element, see Bauckham, "Use of Apocalyptic Traditions"; D. E. Aune, "Apocalypse of John and Palestinian Apocalyptic."

20. Justin, *Dial.* 81 (*ANF* 1:240); Irenaeus, *Her.* 5.30.1 (*ANF* 1:558).

from Jerusalem around A.D. 70.[21] The grammar and style of the Revelation differ markedly from the Fourth Gospel and from the three short epistles ascribed to John.[22] But choice of genre has an impact on style, and the pen that put down the Apocalypse may not have been that of the secretary who brushed up the Gospel (John 21:24), even if both writings well from a single genius as their fountainhead.[23] No one has been able to improve on Irenaeus's information for the date: "That was seen no very long time since, but almost in our own day, towards the end of Domitian's reign [i.e. A.D. 96]."[24]

Who are the "servants" of Jesus Christ for whom the revelation was made (1:1)? Conventional opening and closing matter of a Greco-Roman letter supplies bookends for the prophecy (1:4–9; 22:21). Insofar as the document is an epistle, it is addressed to Christian congregations in seven cities of old western

---

21. Irenaeus, *Her.* 2.22.5 (*ANF* 1:392); Clement of Alexandria, *Rich Man* 42 (*ANF* 2:603); Eusebius *Eccl. Hist.* 3.1.1; 3.20.8–9; 3.31.3; 5.20.6; 5.24.16.

22. The classic study of the idiosyncratic language of the Revelation was Charles, *Revelation*, 1.cxvii–clix. See the further precisions in Aune, *Revelation*, 1.clx–ccxi. On semiticisms in the Greek of the Apocalypse, see the debate among Thompson, *Apocalypse and Semitic Syntax*; Porter, "Language of the Apocalypse"; and Schmidt, "Semitisms in Revelation."

23. Fuller consideration of the authorship of the Revelation: Charles, *Revelation*, xxix–l; Aune, *Revelation*, 1.xlvii–lvi; Mounce, *Revelation*, 8–15; Beale, *Revelation*, 34–36; Osborne, *Revelation*, 2–6.

24. Irenaeus, *Her.* 5.30.3 (*ANF* 1:559–60). Alternative proposals for a date are legion, often intertwined with literalistic interpretations of 17:10–11 leading to conclusions that key parts of the document, at least, were produced in the reigns of Claudius, Nero, or Vespasion. Some posit multiple levels of editing. The more complex compositional hypotheses are also the more speculative. Roman provincial coins from the time of Domitian provide indirect confirmation of the traditional view. Franz, "Propaganda, Coins and Revelation."

Asia Minor: Ephesus, Smyrna, Pergamum, Thyatira, Sardis, Philadelphia, and Laodicea (1:11; cf. 2:1, 8, 12, 18; 3:1, 7, 14). All seven sites have been identified by archaeologists in Turkey, and are easy to find on a good historical map of Roman Anatolia. Each was a thriving regional center at the time of writing.[25]

If the Revelation was a communiqué for its time, sent by a man of antiquity to hearers of antiquity about common concerns, then we have an important guideline for interpretation. Referents for the array of symbols must be sought, in the first instance, in the shared milieu of author and readers.[26] Knowing, for example, that Rome was the imperial city at the time and was popularly dubbed the city of "seven hills" due to its topography,[27] we can make the identification when an angel drops the clues that the seven-headed beast represents "seven mountains on which the woman is seated" and the whore herself "is the great city which has dominion over the kings of the earth" (17:9, 18).

This criterion also rules out errant interpretations. How would it have fortified John's readers in their Roman-Anatolian environment, if the two hundred thousand thousand cavalry of the sixth trumpet (9:16) had been meant to depict yellow hordes of Communist Chinese militiamen allegedly being mobilized toward the end of the twentieth century for an attack on the Middle East; or if the ten horns of the dragon and of the beast (12:3; 13:1) signified the nations of the emerging European Common Market of the 1970s?[28] Not respect for the verbal

---

25. Hemer, *Letters to Seven Churches*; Worth, *Seven Cities and Greco-Asian Culture*; *Seven Cities and Roman Culture*.

26. Bauckham, *Climax of Prophecy*, 174–79.

27. For example, in Horace, *Carmen saeculare* line 7; Suetonius, *Domitian* 4. A collection of ancient Greek texts referring to the "hills" of Rome: Langdon, "Classifying Rome's Hills."

28. Lindsey, *Late Great Planet*, 81–97. Since *The Late Great Planet Earth* was written, the European Union has gained an excess of ten

inerrancy of the predictions, but a disregard for the relationship between the author and his target audience, and a myopic egocentrism that expects his message to shoot straight past them on its way to us, foment such far-fetched conjectures.

> 5. *The message of the book of Revelation was not exhausted in its first-century setting, and remains relevant for believers of later times and other places.*

Although a careful reading takes its starting point from the original rhetorical situation, interpretation need not stop there. One reason why the early Christians canonized this book is because they found in it abiding truths to nourish believers in every age.

In the course of many centuries of study and commentary, several main lines of opinion formed regarding the time of fulfillment of John's visions. According to those who favor a *preterist* approach, all came to pass—or, in the view of some critics, failed to do so—within a few decades of the time of writing (from the Latin *praeter* "past"). To illustrate, preterists typically take the beast to be the Roman emperor. *Historicists* suppose that John was given a preview of church history between the first and second Comings of Christ. On this view, the locusts and horses of chapter 9 might represent the "Turks" that threatened eastern Europe during the Middle Ages. Or the beast might be identified with the Renaissance papacy, as in the outlook of the Protestant reformers. A *futurist* school looks for fulfillment only in the last days. Not until the rise of a global Antichrist will the beast have come. *Idealists* straddle all three views, contending that the symbols portray abstract, perennial ideas behind historical realia. The beast figure, for idealists, depicts human

---

nations in any case. Critique of Lindsey's approach: Bacchiocchi, *Lindsey's Jigsaw*.

government whenever and wherever it is demonically inspired to oppose the church.[29]

Overall the best solution, I shall argue in chapters four and xix, is to give priority to the ancient setting (preterism), recognizing that the language has a fullness that points to the apocalyptic end of history (futurism), idealism forming the bond that unites the two. John perceived, operating in the personages and events of his own locale, forces that would culminate in the end of the world. More precisely, he saw no interval between the decade of the nineties and the final cataclysm, and wrote—hyperbolically, we would say—in his own temporal frame as though the final things were taking place. Indeed, it is characteristic of the biblical prophets that their eye discerns the ultimate principles at stake in the particulars of their immediate situation, principles that often surface again later, in other particulars beyond their own.

If pagan zeal at Pergamum for worship of the emperor (see chapter two) had led to a riot in which one Antipas, a Christian, was lynched for his refusal to take part and became an isolated martyr (2:13), even as John himself had been banished to the island of Patmos for the word of God (1:9), the Antichrist of the latter days had begun to move and the great tribulation was under way (1:9; 2:9, 10; 7:14). Hence John's urgency: "The time is near" (1:3). We, from a later vantage point, can see in retrospect

29. On these four schools of interpretation, see further Tenney, *Interpreting Revelation*, 135–46. The historicist view is dropped as largely discredited today but the other three are represented in Pate, *Four Views on Revelation*—covering preterism, idealism, and two variants of dispensationalism, both futurist. Broader analysis of many avenues of interpretation: Lumsden, *Then the End Will Come*; Suggit, *Oecumenius on Apocalypse*; Backus, *Reformation Readings of the Apocalypse*; Newport, *Apocalypse and Millennium*; Böcher, *Johannesapokalypse*; Wainwright, *Mysterious Apocalypse*; Kovacs and Rowland, *Revelation*.

that the end did not come. But Antipas was a prototype of later Christians who were slain in waves of persecutions. The clash between the world-system and God's faithful ones goes on until God will stand up to vindicate them. John's call to hold fast in the struggle sounds down the corridors of time.

6. *The thesis of the Apocalypse is that God, acting through Jesus Christ, is the Sovereign of history from creation to consummation.*

The gist of the book is adumbrated in the superscription. That God gave the revelation to Jesus Christ to show to his servants, indicates the divine source and agency not only of its literary contents, but of the actual events to which the book points. It lays out a plan originating in heaven concerning "what must soon take place" (1:1). God has predetermined the outcome of history, and has ordained the woes that are coming on the earth and the very machinations of his antagonists, to serve his good ends. It is a story that will lead the people of God past alluring worldly pleasures and through the most harrowing darkness on their way to eternal light. Lest they lose heart or lose their way, he wants to vouchsafe to his servants special knowledge of the end of the story in outline, so that they will endure and enter into the bliss he has in store for them. This theology of history in grand panorama is designed to insure their future salvation by taking them into God's confidence, before their encounter with either Harlot or Beast should place them in peril, so as to orient their trust and perseverance towards him whose counsel prevails and is shot through with unalloyed joy.[30]

Equipped with these assumptions, let us take some topical soundings into what is for many the most difficult book in the Bible, and see what further sense we can make of it.

30. Gilbertson, *God and History*, 45–142.

2

Situation of the Recipients

IF JOHN addressed his prophecy to a group of urban churches in Asia Minor in the mid 90s A.D., then it had a well defined historical setting that can help direct our attention to points of special emphasis in the book.

Asia was richer in urban centers than any other province of the Roman empire.[1] The list of recipient churches for the Revelation (1:11) traces a semi-circular route on the map clockwise following the ancient roads.[2] It starts from Ephesus and moves northwards along the coast as far as Pergamum, then curves round inland to Laodicea to the southeast of Ephesus (chaps. 2–3).

Ephesus, with a population estimated at 200,000,[3] was among the largest metropolitan areas in the empire, trailing only Rome, Alexandria of Egypt, and Syrian Antioch. Paul and his associates, using Ephesus as their base, had evangelized the province of Asia about four decades earlier, in the early 50s (Acts 19:1–10; cf. Col 2:1; 4:12–16). Christianity continued to burgeon, even if heresies threatened to infiltrate some of the churches (Col 2:8–19; 1 Tim 1:3–4, 19–20; 4:1–3; 6:20), and

1. *Encyclopedia of the Early Church* (ed. Di Berardino), 1.85, sv. "Asia."

2. McRay, *Archaeology*, 243–44.

3. McRay, *Archaeology*, 250.

anti-Christian sentiment grew warm among some pagans (1 Peter 1:1; 4:1–4; 5:8–10).[4]

When Roman armies quashed the Jewish uprising in Palestine and sacked Jerusalem in A.D. 70, their blow dispersed, along with militant Jews, many of the Jewish Christians who had made up the oldest and perhaps the most populous regional church. By the end of the first century, although there were pockets of Christian converts dotting Italy, Macedonia, Greece, Syria, Palestine, and Egypt, the largest and densest concentration of Christians in the world were in Roman Asia.[5] The seven churches of the Revelation represented the cradle of Christianity as the church passed into the second century.

But seductions and pressures were increasing for Christians to participate in the affluence of the empire, to compromise on matters of moral conduct, and to support the official state religion.

ROMAN PROSPERITY

Under Caesar Augustus (27 B.C.–A.D. 14), the lands encircling the Mediterranean had begun to enjoy a period of prolonged peace and prosperity known as the *Pax Romana* ("Roman Peace") that lasted through the early centuries A.D. and attained its apogee towards the end of the second. During the first century, Roman armies were invincible. The romanization of Spain was well under way,[6] and Britain was annexed to the empire.[7] Borders had secure guards as far as the Danube.[8] An efficient road system underwent extensions and improvements. Conditions were fair

4. Trebilco, *Early Christians in Ephesus*.
5. Aharoni and Avi-Yonah, *Atlas*, p. 166, map 263.
6. Sutherland, *Romans in Spain*.
7. Suetonius, *Claudius* 17.
8. Suetonius, *Tiberius* 18.

for industry and trade to advance.⁹ New building projects in Rome were representative of those in many other cities: the first century saw the making of roads, aqueducts, fora, the *Circus Vaticanus* where Christians later became victims of wild beasts, and the *Amphitheatrum Flavium*, better known to posterity as the Colosseum.¹⁰ Revelation 18:12–13 itemizes various Roman luxury wares that pandered to exotic tastes.

While the empire as a whole had an underdeveloped economy that saw only modest growth in the two centuries after Augustus,¹¹ Asia Minor rose to a level not matched before or since.¹² Ephesus, for its part, was mistress of western Anatolia, situated on the coast where the Caÿster river empties into the Aegean Sea, and affording good access to one of the chief overland highways between Greece and Cilicia. Strabo (64/63 B.C.– A.D. 21) considered Ephesus the major center of commerce west of the Taurus range.¹³ The temple of Artemis (Acts 19:23–41), one of the seven wonders of the world, held a place among the leading banks of the empire.¹⁴ As the proconsuls kept their headquarters at Ephesus, it was the real capital of the province of Asia, even if the title probably still belonged to Pergamum.¹⁵ Inscriptions show that Thyatira (2:18–29) was known for its trade guilds of workers in wool, linen, leather, and bronze, of

9. Davis, *Influence of Wealth in Rome*, 37–151.

10. Scullard, "Rome (History)," 930–31; Richmond and Castagnoli, "Rome (Topography)," 935–36.

11. Garnsey and Saller, *Roman Empire*, 51–63.

12. Dudley, *Civilization of Rome*, 195–96.

13. Strabo, *Geographica* 12.8.15 (LCL, vol. 5, pp. 508–9).

14. Dudley, *Civilization of Rome*, 195.

15. Calder and Cook, "Ephesus," 387. Colin Hemer points out that Pergamum remained the religious capital of Asia even if the rivalry of Ephesus and Smyrna in administration and finance had eroded its claim to be the political capital. Hemer, *Letters to Seven Churches*, 82.

tanners, potters, bakers, tailors, slave dealers, and dyers (cf. Acts 16:14).[16] Sardis (3:1–6) minted coins, and bits of jewelry have been found in its cemeteries.[17] Laodicea was the wealthiest town in Phrygia, renowned for its exports of black wool and tunics, and for its banking.[18]

In this busy environment, it was tempting for Christians to compromise their standards by joining a trade association that performed idolatrous rites to a tutelary pagan deity at its meetings,[19] or simply to make the accumulation of goods the goal of daily life. Of the mercantile society of the Roman Empire the prophetic voice warns: "Come out of her, my people, lest you take part in her sins, lest you share in her plagues" (18:4).

BREAKDOWN IN MORAL BEHAVIOR

Waxing affluence brought vice in its train. In debauchery, as in economic development, Rome set the trend. From the racy novels of Petronius in the first century to Apuleius in the second, we get vignettes of traditional sexual mores in deterioration at the upper crust.[20] Stage productions became offensively lewd, cloaking appeal to prurient interests in the guise of myths concerning the capers of gods and goddesses.[21] Crowds in the circuses made ever

---

16. Ramsay, *Letters to Seven Churches*, 239.

17. Mounce, *Revelation*, 92.

18. Dudley, *Civilization of Rome*, 196; Mounce, *Revelation*, 107.

19. Kraybill, *Imperial Cult and Commerce*; Harland, "Honouring the Emperor."

20. Petronius, *The Satyricon*; Apuleius, *The Golden Ass*.

21. Lucian, *De saltatione* 37–61 (LCL, vol. 5, pp. 248–65); Tertullian, *De spectaculis* (*ANF* 3:79–91); Augustine, *Civitas Dei* 2.8, 27 (*NPNF*[2] 2:27, 41). Tucker, *Life in the Roman World*, 268–73; Carcopino, *Daily Life in Rome*, 228–31.

more bloodthirsty demands for gladiatorial spectacles.[22] From time to time the general peace was disturbed by news of assassinations and coups at the highest level, such as the rapid series of three emperors in the wake of Nero's death in A.D. 68/69. Domitian became tyrannical toward the end of his reign, and eliminated shocking numbers of suspected personal enemies.[23]

John inveighs against the blasphemies, the murders, the immoralities, the lies, and the sorceries that abounded in Roman society, warning that God will judge the doers of such acts and exclude them from the heavenly city that is coming (9:21; 16:21; 21:8, 27; 22:15). But more provocative to him were encroachments of moral degradation on the life of some of the churches.

At least three of the seven churches were feeling the effects of a religious movement our author calls the Nicolaitans (2:6, 14–15; cf. v. 20). Etymologically the name means "people-conquerors," suggesting they were making inroads in Christian circles. Their teachers seem to have twisted Paul's original gospel of justification by faith into a libertarian doctrine to the effect that Christians are free to live like their unbelieving neighbors with impunity. In particular, the false teachers egged on Christians to participate in idolatrous rituals despite Paul's prohibition (cf. 1 Cor 10:1–22), and to involve themselves in unspecified forms of lasciviousness. The prophet thunders that Christ hates these works (2:6), and will soon wield the sword of his mouth (2:16) to slay those who practice such things (2:23).

---

22. Tucker, *Life in the Roman World*, 280–88; Carcopino, *Daily Life in Rome*, 231–47.

23. Suetonius, *Domitian* 10–15; Tacitus, *Agricola* 2, 39–43; Dio Cassius, *Epitome* 67.14.1–3.

HERO VENERATION IN ASIA

At some point during the reign of Domitian (81–96), the city of Ephesus honored him by dedicating a temple to him just off its main, upper square, complete with a colossus of him 4.8 meters high. Similar dedications in many other cities at about the same time attest that the whole province followed suit.[24] This wave of enthusiasm for the cult of the Roman ruler may have been the occasion for the Apocalypse.

To pay divine honors to rulers, in acknowledgment of their power and in gratitude for favors bestowed, had been customary in parts of the Ancient Near East since time immemorial. Alexander the Great, hailed as son of the sun-god Amon-Ra by the Egyptian priest of Ammon at Siwa in 331 B.C., fancied the idea and soon demanded recognition of his divinity from the cities of Greece and Asia Minor.[25] When these places came under Roman control in the first century B.C., it was natural for the conquered peoples to transfer their sycophancy to their new overlords.

Ephesus had a sacrificial cult and priesthood to Publius Servilius Isauricus, Roman consul of Asia 46–44 B.C., even into the imperial era.[26] Octavian (later to become Caesar Augustus), shortly after his ascendancy at Actium (31 B.C.), allowed the Ephesians to erect a sacred precinct for the worship of the genius of Rome and the deified Julius Caesar.[27] The first temple in Asia dedicated to the living Augustus, however, was at Pergamum in 29 B.C., pictured on numerous coins (cf. "Satan's throne" [?] Rev 2:13).[28] In Asia Minor as a whole, thirteen imperial temples or

24. Price, *Rituals and Power*, 123–24, 140, 187, 198.

25. Edson, "Ruler-Cult. Greek," 938–39.

26. Oster, "Ephesus," 548.

27. Oster, "Ephesus," 544.

28. Price, *Rituals and Power*, 95; Hemer, *Letters to Seven Churches*, 84; Yarbro Collins, "Satan's Throne."

sanctuaries were built before the turn of the era, ten more before A.D. 50, an additional seven before A.D. 100, yet another fifteen before A.D. 150.[29]

From Julius onwards, the Roman senate voted divine honors to each caesar on his death.[30] The first emperor to demand acclaim as divine during his lifetime was Gaius, and he was regarded as mad.[31] By the end of the first century A.D., traditional western qualms about deifying men were in abeyance.[32] Domitian, on gaining the throne, dedicated a large temple to Jupiter "with his own effigy in the lap of the god,"[33] and later suffered devotees to address him as "Lord and God (*dominus et deus*)" (cf. "blasphemies," Rev 13:1, 5).[34]

Typically an imperial temple had an altar and a priest (ἀρχιερεύς [*archiereus*], or *flamen*) with helpers, and often a statue of the reigning emperor for people to adore (cf. "image for the beast," Rev 13:14).[35] Some statues, kept in darkened chambers for oracular encounters, were equipped with clever mechanical devices to move the jaws, and priests who practiced ventriloquism from behind curtains made them converse with suppliants (Rev 13:15).[36] Theatrical shows could make use of

29. Price, *Rituals and Power*, 84.

30. Hammond, "Ruler-Cult. Roman," 939.

31. Suetonius, *Gaius Caligula* 22, 27, 33, 35, 50–52.

32. The encroachment of eastern ruler-worship on the Latin west is detailed in Fishwick, *Imperial Cult in the Latin West*.

33. Tacitus, *Histories* 3.74.

34. Suetonius, *Domitian* 13; Martial, *Epigrams* 5.8; cf. 2.91; 4.1; 5.1, etc.

35. Ferguson, *Backgrounds*, 164.

36. Lucian, *Alexander the False Prophet* 12, 26. Many other examples: Scherrer, "Signs and Wonders," 601–4.

elaborate stage machinery to simulate thunder and lightning (Rev 13:13).[37]

On festival days, the high priest, dressed in purple and wearing a unique crown adorned with as many as fifteen miniature busts of members of the emperor's family,[38] would follow a large statue of the emperor in solemn parade through the main streets to the city square, accompanied by white-robed, garlanded youths bearing incense. All houses along the thoroughfare were required by law to set out sacrifices of incense on small private altars by their doors, or to hang wreaths.[39] Failure to conform would be noticeable, and might bring suspicion of treason, reproaches, or legal accusations, resulting in confiscation of property, imprisonment, or execution.[40] There is a modicum of evidence that at some point in the closing decades of the first century, trading in the marketplace of Ephesus was restricted to those who would perform small acts of acknowledgement to the imperial statue on their way in or out (cf. "the mark," 13:16–17).[41] These measures brought pressure to bear on Christians, whose consciences were at liberty to worship only the one God.

Proconsuls of Asia took their prerogatives seriously. Though we have no record from the 90s A.D., we can gauge their attitudes by reference to Tacitus, the famous historian, who

---

37. Julius Pollux, *Onomasticon* 4.130; Heron of Alexandria, *Pneumatica* 20.4; note also Heron's entire treatise *On Automata-making*, on the construction of devices for working miracles in temples. These references and others are in Scherrer, "Signs and Wonders," 604–10.

38. Yamauchi, *Archaeology in Asia Minor*, 110; Price, *Rituals and Power*, 170–71, photograph plates 1a, 2f.

39. Price, *Rituals and Power*, 108–12, 123–24, 129, 189, 198.

40. Tertullian *De idololatria* 13–16 (*ANF* 3:68–71); Price, *Rituals and Power*, 123.

41. Judge, "Mark of the Beast," 158–60.

served as *quindecimvir* at the Secular Games of Domitian in A.D. 88 and was proconsul of Asia A.D. 113–116, about twenty years after the Revelation was written.[42] His esteem for Domitian's imperial successor is given in the phrase, "the deified Nerva" (*divi Nervae*);[43] his opinion of Christians, in a fragment where he approves of Titus's destruction of the Jerusalem temple as necessary "in order to wipe out more completely the religion of the Jews and the Christians . . . The Christians had grown out of the Jews: if the root were destroyed, the stock would easily perish."[44] That there was plenty of civic animus against Christianity in Asia is apparent from preserved correspondences between Pliny, governor of Bithynia A.D. 112, and Trajan;[45] and between Serenius Granianus, proconsul of Asia until A.D. 122, and Hadrian,[46] both asking the emperor how the local governor should respond to numerous informers against Christians. For some of the slanderous information, local Jews appear to have been responsible (2:9; 3:9).[47]

The social climate in Asia being what it was, it is scarcely necessary to settle the debate among scholars about how to reconcile references to the persecution of Christians in the Apocalypse

42. Clifford H. Moore, "Introduction," to Tacitus' *Histories* (LCL, Tacitus, vol. 2, p. vii).

43. Tacitus, *Hist.* 1.1.

44. Tacitus, *Hist.*, Fragments 2 (LCL, Tacitus, vol. 3, p. 221).

45. Pliny, *Epistles* 10, "To Trajan," 96.

46. Justin, *First Apology* appendix (*ANF* 1:186).

47. Lambrecht, "Jewish Slander." This traditional explanation of Revelation 2:9 and 3:9 is far more likely than recent, politically correct, proposals. Frankfurter, "Jews?," suggests John's "Jews" are Pauline converts not ritually pure in John's Jewish-Christian eyes. McKelvey, "Jews in Revelation" tries to make them out to be non-Christian Jews who, like the Johannine Christians, were in danger of losing their distinctive character through accommodation to paganism.

with the fact that Domitian himself probably did not instigate a general persecution of the church.[48] Given the background, we have every reason to suppose that Antipas was a Christian who had suffered death at the hands of an irate mob in Pergamum not long before the Apocalypse was written (2:13). John foresaw further imprisonments (2:10) and martyrdoms in the near future (6:9–11; 11:7; 13:7, 10; 14:13; 16:6; 17:6; 19:2; 20:4).

FASCINATION WITH ROMAN POWER

The wish to exploit growing material prosperity, the willingness to slacken moral discipline, and the fear of stigmatization by society, were not always separate temptations but could blend to reinforce each other. Officers of the imperial cult could foster flattery of the emperor by enforcing conditions on trade in the market place (13:16–17). Uniting all three interests was the lure of Roman culture.

Rome's overpowering magnetism can be illustrated by a description of the triumphal march held in A.D. 70 or 71 to celebrate her military victory over the Jews in Palestine, as witnessed and recorded by Flavius Josephus. Hundreds of thousands of people massed along the roads, fora, Circus and theaters of

---

48. Eusebius remembered Domitian as the second of the emperors after Nero to persecute the church (*Eccl. Hist.* 3.17; 3.19–20). Although a few prominent Christians may have suffered among others during Domitian's reign of terror, there is no unambiguous evidence from contemporary sources for an imperial decree concerning Christians as such. See Newman, "Fallacy of Domitian Hypothesis"; Bruce, *History*, 412; Bell, "Date of Apocalypse"; Collins, *Crisis and Catharsis*; Thompson, *Revelation and Empire*, 95–132, 171–85. On the other hand, there is ample local evidence of popular fervor for the imperial cult in Asia Minor, which might have worked against the Christians. See Fiorenza, *Vision of a Just World*, 55; Friesen, *Twice Neokoros*; *Imperial Cults and the Apocalypse*; Slater, "Social Setting"; De Villiers, "Persecution."

the city to see the procession. It began with displays of unbelievable quantities of crafted items in silver, gold, and ivory; of tapestries; and of gems "swept by in such profusion as to correct our erroneous supposition that any of them was rare." Then came caparisoned animals from all over the world, followed by Jewish captives of war selected for their handsome figures, decked out in fine apparel to hide any wounds. Prominent among the captives was Simon son of Gioras, who had been leader of the Jewish resistance. Next was a pageant of moving stages, each three or four stories high, with broad paintings on their sides depicting the episodes of the campaign, together with several naval vessels. More spoils followed "in promiscuous heaps," the most interesting to Josephus being the sacred Menorah and a copy of the Torah plundered from the temple. At last the generals Vespasian and Titus rode by, clad in purple robes and crowned with laurel, with Domitian mounted on a steed beside them. The procession made its way to the temple of Jupiter Capitolinus. There, at the northeastern end of the Forum, Simon suffered a scourging and was executed, to "shouts of universal applause." After the customary prayers and sacrifices, the leading men withdrew to banquets at the palace and in private homes for the rest of the day.[49]

Of this sort of grandeur the cities of Asia had their own more modest share. Ephesus, for example, during the first century A.D. gained several Neocorate temples, several gymnasium-bath complexes, and at least three aqueducts connected to two new public fountains—centers respectively for colorful religious festivals, public athletic contests, and general socializing.[50]

At a time when Christians were at risk of being carried off their feet by the glamour of Roman culture exported to Asia, God gave the Revelation to John to stabilize their view of real-

49. Josephus, *J.W.* 7.120–57.
50. Oster, "Ephesus," 547.

ity.[51] Life and dynamism, substance and radiance, excitement and happiness, are not to be found in a rapacious culture upon which God has already pronounced condemnation. They are to be found in God and his will.

TRUE POWER AND TRUE WEALTH

While Rome presented her might and glory to the senses, the reign of God was a matter of faith, silent and hidden, something that did not seem to have much of an impact on human experience, whether that of the nations being devoured by imperial dominion, or that of an individual Christian languishing in a municipal prison. The Apocalypse, therefore, is an "unveiling" of those invisible realities that are in fact definitive, to put Roman pomp in the shade.[52] Through John's descriptions of what befell him in the Spirit, the reader is led through a series of quite sensory experiences—sights, sounds, smells—designed to drive home the true state of affairs.

To a Roman like Tacitus, Jesus was but a Jewish malefactor who got himself crucified and disappeared from the course of events.[53] To John, Jesus is revealed as an imposing heavenly priest-king who has conquered death and now lives forever, whose face shines like the sun, whose voice roars like a waterfall, and who holds the churches in the palm of his right hand (1:12–20). Though the whole of western civilization was falling into line to offer adulation and sacrifice to the emperor (13:4, 7–8), God and the Lamb are shown to sit on a throne transcending the universe, receiving rightful praise from rank upon rank of seraphim, archangels, angels in their myriads of myriads,

---

51. Friesen, "Myth and Resistance," 281–313.
52. DeSilva, "Construction of Counter-Cosmos," 47–61.
53. Tacitus, *Annals* 15.44.

and every living thing on or under the earth (chaps 4–5).[54] If Rome was pursuing a program of conquest and aggrandizement, God holds in his hand the book in which are written the woes decreed to come upon the empire leading to its utter collapse and replacement by God's eternal kingdom, a plan the Lamb is about to enact (5:1–5; 6:1–17; 8:1–5; etc.). However awash Rome may be in the riches of plundered peoples, all of them and more besides are to be offered to God and to the Lamb (5:12).

Not only does the Revelation manifest who is the Potentate of potentates (1:5; 17:14; 19:16), it also portrays Rome and its blandishments in the light of God's evaluation. Her political institutions are a savage monster straight from the pit of hell (11:7; 13:1–10; 17:8–14). Her imperial religion is another brute like the first, lying, ruthless, vomiting frogs out of its mouth (13:11–18; 16:13). Her commercial and social engine looks attractive on the surface but is a besotted whore (17:3–6, 15–18; chap. 18). All are destined to perdition (14:6—19:21).

God's downtrodden faithful, on the other hand, are slated to have their fortunes completely reversed. Rising from martyrdom to rule with Christ till the end of the age (20:4–6), they will become his dear bride (19:1–10; 21:9–10), his inner sanctum (21:11–22), a body of kings who will inherit his new creation for ever and ever (21:23—22:5).

ETHICAL TENOR OF THE PROPHECY

From beginning to end, the burden of the Apocalypse is therefore a summons to persevere in doing God's will in the midst of a commonwealth attuned to this heady world.

A blessing in the prescript invites readers to "keep what is written" in the book (1:3). The epistolary opening bristles with encouraging theological truths (1:4–8). The audience have

54. Morton, "Glory to God and Lamb," 89–109.

entered with the author into the paradox of tribulation and kingdom, and are one with him in "patient endurance" (1:9). It is reassuring that the glorious Christ holds the churches in his hand (1:16, 20). Each message to one of the seven churches analyzes the strong and weak points in its attitudes and conduct, and either chides or comforts the church accordingly (chaps. 2–3).

No reader will want to miss out on joining the everlasting hymn to God and to the Lamb (5:8–14; cf. 7:9–14; 14:2–3; 15:3–4; 19:1–8). Among afflictions soon coming on the empire (chap. 6), God's blueprint provides for an exact number of those who persist in their witness to the word of God to pay for it with their lives, who will be avenged in due course (6:9–11; cf. 11:4–13). God's chosen are promised his protective seal against his plagues (7:1–8), and coronation as royal priests (7:15–17; cf. 1:6; 20:6); the rest of humankind will suffer for flouting God's commands (9:20–21). Those who keep God's commandments and testify to Jesus will be objects of the wrath of the dragon for a short time only (12:17). When John sees the beast come up out of the sea and begin to wreak violence on the saints, he issues calls for their endurance and faith (13:10–11; 14:12), and pronounces a benediction on the ones who will die (14:13). God's elect abstain from the wantonness of the day and have no lie in their mouths (14:4–5). Conquerors will sing of God's deliverance (15:2–4). The empire will attack the saints, but they are to hang on to their garments of good behavior lest they be ashamed in the day of judgment (16:13–16; cf. 19:8). They are the faithful (17:14). They must exit from Babylon in the confidence that God will judge in their favor over against the kings of the earth who commit fornication with her (18:4, 9, 20). The Lamb's bride prepares for her wedding feast by putting on the fine linen of righteous deeds (19:7–9). Faithfulness to the bitter end will be amply rewarded: Christian confessors whose heads have rolled under the Roman ax will live to reign with Christ and will be immune to the second death (20:4, 6). Sins that will exclude their practitioners from life in the new heaven and new earth include temptations to which John's readership are exposed (21:8, 27; 22:10–15).

This accent on maintaining Christian behavior in an age of decay pervades the Revelation and comes through in special themes:

(1) frequent exhortations to "hear" what is being said (1:3; 2:7, 11, 17, 29; 3:3, 6, 13, 20, 22; 13:9; 22:18);

(2) "keeping"—what is written, or God's word, or the commandments, or one's garments (1:3; 2:26; 3:3, 8, 10; 12:17; 14:12; 16:15; 22:7, 9);

(3) "works," either good or bad, as the criterion according to which God will judge people (2:2, 5, 6, 19 [twice], 22, 23, 26; 3:1, 2, 8, 15; 9:20; 14:13; 16:11; 18:6; 20:12, 13; 22:12);

(4) promises of rewards for those who "conquer" by holding to their testimony in the face of the conquering beast (2:7, 11, 17, 26; 3:5, 12, 21; 12:11; 15:2; 21:7; cf. 5:5);

(5) "white" garments as a symbol of moral excellence (3:4–5, 18; 6:11; 7:9, 13; 19:14).

SUMMARY

John's tone in the Apocalypse is grave. He sees the powers of a doomed world-system trying to suck the churches into a maelstrom, whether by enticement or by fear. What is at stake is nothing less than whether professing Christians are staying the course to inherit eternal life. Only if they see reality as God sees it will they be braced to make it through the rigors that lie ahead of them. And only if they are faithful to the end will they be saved.

3

Literary Structure

As a piece of literature, the book of Revelation is well crafted. It makes more extensive use of patterns and devices than any other book in the biblical canon. All who have closely studied the Apocalypse share a sense that it is artfully constructed, and that a good deal of the meaning lies in the way the parts interact. Unfortunately, almost as many outlines of the book exist as do commentators on it.[1]

One reason for such disparity is that decisions about literary form are often mixed up with judgments about the meanings of the symbols; and, as we saw in our first chapter, the references may be variously taken to be to the author's day (preterism), to the progress of church history (historicism), to the end of the world (futurism), or to abstract ideas (idealism). Some read the book as a linear chronicle of events, usually historicists or futurists. For example, the sequence of the seven seals (chap. 6) may be thought to continue in the seven trumpets (chaps. 8–9). Other readers, often preterists or idealists, find a simple core of events replayed several times from different points of view, in cyclical (or conically spiral) recapitulations. So the trumpets (chaps. 8–9) and the bowls (chap. 16), at least, might cover the

---

1. On the structure, many keen observations are to be found in Collins, *Combat Myth*, 5–55; Fiorenza, *Justice and Judgment*, 159–80; Bauckham, "Structure." See the reviews of several outlines for the book proposed by other scholars, in Beale, *Revelation*, 108–51; Tavo, "Structure."

same ground in parallel.[2] We shall return later to the question of plot development.

Another hindrance to clarity is the fact that the chapter divisions as they have come down to us (probably from Stephen Langton, Paris, early 1200s) do not always correspond very well to the natural segments of the narrative, especially in chapters 6–22. For example, the head of chapter 8 breaks up the series of seven seals, which ends properly at 8:5.

The analysis that follows takes its cues from the surface phenomena of the text, keeping their content or reference a secondary consideration, and ignoring the chapter and verse divisions. It assumes that the literary configuration is meant to steer rather than befuddle the reader, and so, however complex it may seem at first, should yield sense once its underlying rationale is discovered. Rather than review the process by which I arrived at my conclusions—which is impossible to recall after some decades of continuing study and reflection—I shall lay out the results. In the nature of the case, large literary designs are best surveyed as wholes. Either they fit the material, or they do not.

PRESCRIPT (1:1–11) AND POSTSCRIPT (22:6–21)

The prescript and the postscript stand together apart from the rest. After a formal superscription (1:1–3), the book adopts the conventions of a Greco-Roman letter opening. Author and recipients are named, with a greeting (1:4–5a). There follow, in place of the usual prayer for the recipients, a doxology and a summary oracle (1:5b–6, 7–8). In 1:9–11, a brief note of the author's

---

2. This was the view of the earliest commentator on the book of Revelation, Victorinus of Pettau (*d.* between 284 and 305). See his commentary on Revelation 7 (*ANF* 7.352). Seminal in sowing this view among many twentieth-century commentators was Hendriksen, *More Than Conquerors*, esp. 22–31.

circumstances with a specific list of intended recipients (cf. v. 4) rounds off the sub-unit and provides a transition to the body.

A reprise of the basic matter of 1:1–3 indicates the opening (22:6b–8a) of the postscript, which is studded with motifs that reflect the prescript. In both, an angel is the agent of the revelation (22:6, 8b–9; cf. 1:1). A final instruction not to seal up the prophecy corresponds to the earlier command to write it down (22:10; cf. 1:11). That the time is "near" (22:10; cf. 1:3) or "soon" (22:6, 12, 20; cf. 1:1) is stressed, as before. Again Christ's second coming is promised, followed by an "Amen" (22:7, 12, 20; cf. 1:7), and the deity is designated as "Alpha and Omega" (22:13; cf. 1:8). Those who keep what is written are blessed (22:7, 14; cf. 1:3). Jesus is identified as the giver of the revelation (22:16; cf. 1:1). The grace is repeated (22:21; cf. 1:4–5).

Hence a little tripartite chiasm (ABC CBA) comprises 1:1–11 and 22:10–21.

Superscription (1:1–3)	(A)	(C)	Instruction not to seal it up (22:10–11)
Summary oracle (1:7–8)	(B)	(B)	Summary oracle (22:12–13)
Instruction to write (1:9–11)	(C)	(A)	Subscription (22:14–16)

Into this chiasm other matter has been inserted where appropriate. To the epistolary opening are added a greeting and doxology (1:4–6). The conclusion is enhanced by an invitation to "come," with a warning not to tamper with the text (22:17–20); and a concluding grace (22:21).

BODY (1:9—22:9): MAIN SECTIONS

To create a seamless fabric, John has made the end of the prescript overlap with the beginning of the body at 1:9–11. His circumstances, part of the content of epistolary opening matter, are taken up into the first vision. Likewise near the end of the book, the body overlaps with the postscript at 22:6–9, where clauses occur that mark the conclusion of the foregoing vision (21:9—22:9).[3]

Unequal halves make up the body: first, a set of seven oracles for the churches given by an apparition of the glorified Christ on the isle of Patmos (chapters 1–3, excluding the prescript), then a set of visions displayed to John in the temple of heaven, from the throne of God and of the Lamb (chapters 4–22, excluding the postscript). These sections are introduced in the same way, with a "voice like a trumpet" that arrests John's attention (1:10; 4:1). In both cases the author becomes conscious of being "in the Spirit" (1:10; 4:2). He is told to write what he sees, "what is and what is to take place hereafter" (1:19; cf. "what must take place after this," 4:1). By having these similarities, the sections are shown to correspond to each other. The statement "I was in the Spirit" precedes the voice like a trumpet in 1:10, but follows the same voice in 4:1–2, creating another small chiasm (AB BA). This chiasm is a closing device telling the reader not to expect any further announcements by the voice like a trumpet. Structurally it means that chapters 1–3 (excluding the prescript) and chapters 4–22 (excluding the postscript) are the two and only two main sections of the body. There are no other section markers at this principal level of organization. The main sections are

3. The statement "These words are trustworthy and true" (22:6) rounds off each of the previous two subsections as well (19:9; 21:5; finishing 17:1—19:10 and 19:11—21:8 respectively). Also a second frustrated attempt to worship the revealing angel (22:8b–9; cf. 19:10) closes the material on Lady Jerusalem (21:9—22:9), as it did that on Lady Babylon (17:1—19:10). That these features serve as sectional markers will become clear through the analysis below of the visions in chapters 6–22.

confirmed by the difference in genre between dictated auditory-verbal messages (2–3) and interactive, visionary ones (4–22).[4]

Each major division of the body unfolds from a disclosure of the person of the Lord. The description of Christ in his resurrected and ascended glory (1:12–20) supplies the personal attributes named at the heads of the individual oracles to the churches (2:1, 8, 12, 18; 3:1, 7, 14), thus subordinating the seven messages to their speaker. Likewise, in the course of the throne-vision of God in chapters 4–5, a scroll is seen in God's right hand (5:1–8), the breaking of whose seals by the Lamb initiates the series of visions in chapters 6–22. In this way, the visions that follow concerning the denouement of history are shown to be the fiat of the One who sits on the throne. In both halves, the character of the divine figure(s) determines the nature of what is revealed.

Many factors tie the two main sections together. "Endurance," commended in the written oracles (2:2, 3, 19; 3:10), is also called for in the visions (13:10; 14:12). Christ's threat to come to Pergamum and war against wayward church members with the sword of his mouth (2:12, 16) anticipates the language of Armageddon (19:15, 21). Mention of a "great tribulation" at 2:22 is echoed at 7:14. The theme of keeping one's white garments unsoiled, broached at 3:4, 18, is developed in the longer section (6:11; 7:9, 13; 16:15; 19:14). The keeping of the Philadelphian church from "the hour of trial which is coming on the whole world" (3:10) points toward the plagues of the trumpets and bowls from which God's saints are protected (7:2; 9:4; cf. 16:2, 10). Each message in chapters 2–3 has a special promise for the one who conquers (2:7, 11, 17, 26–28; 3:5,

---

4. A surprising number of proposed structural schemes for the Apocalypse go wrong through failure to observe this fundamental bifurcation of the body.

12, 21). Many of these promises of the first part are elaborated in the second, especially in chapters 20–22.

All of which suggests that the sections consisting of chapters 1–3 and 4–22 are complementary and mutually interpreting. The same essential message that is compressed in the epistolary oracles is expanded in the symbolic visions. Probably the reason why the book's essential content is given twice over is explained by Genesis 41:32: "And the doubling . . . means that the thing is fixed by God, and God will shortly bring it to pass" (cf. Rev 1:1).

ORACLES ADDRESSED TO THE CHURCHES (CHAPTERS 2–3)

A common pattern stamps the seven units in the first section of the body.

1. Command to write to the angel of the church in a given city

2. Statement that the words are those of Christ, betokened by a feature from the preceding representation of him (1:12–20)

3. Commendation of the church for its strong points

4. Notation of the church's unsatisfactory points

5. Bid to repent, together with the consequence, should there be no repentance

6. (7) Invitation to one who has ears, to hear what the Spirit is saying to the churches

7. (6) Promise to the one who conquers (in most cases pointing to chapters 20–22)

Sub-groups of three and of four units stand out, in that items 6 and 7 are reversed in the last four messages (2:28–29; 3:5–6, 12–13, 21–22). In the case of two of the five churches, the notation of unacceptable points is omitted, together with the bid to repent, and instead we find promises of comfort with encouragements to continue in their present virtues (Smyrna, 2:10; Philadelphia, 3:8–11). As we shall see, John also groups the visions of chapters 6–22 into sets of three and four, and of five and two.

SYMBOLIC VISIONS (CHAPTERS 6–22)

Our first task in analyzing the greater portion of the body is to determine how many subsections are demarcated.

Easiest to identify are the enumerated visions: seven seals (6 + 8:1–5)[5], seven trumpets (8:6—9:21 + 11:14–19), and seven bowls (15:5—16:21). Not only the stylized schemes of seven items each, but also a common closing formula, modelled on the "flashes of lightning, and voices and peals of thunder" that characterize the heavenly throne of God (4:5), thrice repeated in the respective seventh units (8:5; 11:19; 16:18), divide the narrative into periods.

Directly appended to the enumerated visions are two further ones (17—19:10, and 21:9—22:9), in that each is introduced by "one of the seven angels who had the seven bowls" (17:1; 21:9). In both instances the angel engages John using the words, "Come, I will show you . . ." (17:2; 21:9). What are shown are two female figures representing polar human communities: a harlot named after the city of Babylon (17:1, 5), and a pure bride named after Jerusalem (21:9, 10). John is "carried" by the angel "in the Spirit," first to a wilderness (17:3), then later to a high mountain (21:10), where he witnesses the final judgment of the one, and the eternal

---

5. Broken references are required owing to John's use of the literary device of "intercalation" or "chain linkage" to mesh together the visions that make up chapters 6–22. On the device, see below, footnote 9. On 8:3–5, see Stefanovic, "Angel at Altar."

glory of the other. A formula signals the close of both subsections: the angel announces, "These are true words of God" (19:9; 22:6), to which John responds by offering worship, which the angel rebuffs (19:10; 22:8–9). These two visions, then, manifest the upshot of the series of seals, trumpets and bowls in antithetical outcomes, the divine sentence on Lady Babylon (17—19:10) and the exaltation of Lady Jerusalem (21:9—22:9). Thus far we have five clearly delineated visions.

Sandwiched between the second and third heptads (the trumpets and the bowls) is the beginning of a special drama having its own characters and motifs (12—14:5 + 14:14—15:4), introduced by the words, "And a great portent appeared in heaven" (12:1). Its plot centers on a cosmic war between the forces of heaven and those of the fallen world (12:7, 17; 13:4, 7) that takes place during a period of three-and-a-half years (12:6, 14; 13:5; cf. 17:10; 20:3). Three antagonists come onto the scene: a dragon (chap. 12), a beast (13:1–10), and a second beast (13:11–18), later called "the false prophet" (cf. 16:13; 19:20; 20:10). To these three stand opposed a corporate protagonist of 144,000 followers of the Lamb (14:1–5). The conflict ends summarily when the earth is reaped by "one like a son of man" (14:14–16) with his angels (14:17–20), followed by a paeon of praise to God for his just judgments, by the humble conquerors (15:2–4).[6]

A similar block of material (19:11—21:8) stands between the fate of the harlot (17:1—19:10) and the exaltation of the bride (21:9—22:9). Heaven opens (19:11) and the combat theme is renewed (19:11, 19; 20:8) with an emphasis on the overthrow of God's enemies. Their order mirrors chiastically that in chapters 12–13, where the dragon was introduced before the beasts: now, first the beast and the false prophet (19:19–21), then the dragon (20:1–10) meet their doom. After a general resurrection and assize

6. Collins, *Combat Myth*, 57–206.

(20:11–15), God establishes a new heaven and a new earth where his covenantal promises come to perfect fulfillment (21:1–8). This subsection closes, like those on its flanks, with "These words are trustworthy and true" (21:5; cf. 19:9; 22:6).

The chiasm, observed by Gaechter in reference to the order of the antagonists,[7] encompasses everything in the two subsections (12—14:5 and 19:11—21:8).

Heavenly woman (12:1–2)	(A)	(D)	Followers of the Rider (19:11–16)
Dragon on the attack (12:3–17)	(B)	(C)	Beasts defeated (19:17–21)
Beasts on the attack (13)	(C)	(B)	Dragon defeated (20:1–10)
Followers of the Lamb (14:1–5; 15:2)	(D)	(A)	Heavenly woman (21:1–8, esp. v. 2)

This chiasm establishes a special relationship between these two subsections of material. The drama that begins to unfold in 12—14:5 is resolved in 19:11—21:8, as the antagonists who were introduced one by one in the former section are overthrown in the latter in reverse order, while the people of God, represented as a celestial woman, are vindicated.

Hence we find seven visions in chapters 6–22.

I. Seven seals (6 + 8:1–5);
II. Seven trumpets (8:6—9:21 + 11:14–19);
III. Combat joined (12:1—14:5 + 14:14—15:4);
IV. Seven bowls (15:5—16:21);
V. Judgment of Babylon (17:1—19:10);
VI. Combat resolved (19:11—21:8);
VII. Glory of Jerusalem (21:9—22:9).

---

7. The chiasm is noted in Massyngberde Ford, *Revelation*, 330, quoting and crediting (but not citing) P. Gaechter.

Visions I, II, IV, V, and VII form a sequence of links, into which III and VI are interpolated. I, II, and IV (seals, trumpets, bowls) have as their issue the antithetical outcomes in V and VII (Babylon, Jerusalem). VI (combat resolved) completes III (combat joined). The chiastic distribution of the III–VI story (combat) among segments of the I–II–IV–V–VII story demonstrates the interrelation of both stories.[8]

Literary clasps string together most of these visions.[9] Before the seventh seal runs its course (8:1, 3–5), angels prepare to blow the trumpets (8:2). Before the last trumpet is blown (11:15–19), the combat epic is introduced as a second, little prophecy within the big prophecy (10) and a précis of its plot is shown (11:1–13). Before the last scene of the first combat section (15:2–4), the bowl-plagues are announced in a portent (15:1). That the seven bowl-plagues are "the last" (15:1) indicates that they conclude what the seals and the trumpets started. Before they terminate, the account leaves the reader dangling in

---

8. The order of the subsections may have numerological significance. The opening of the seals comes first because they initiate the whole narrative sequence. The ordinal of the bowls (IV) doubles, and so intensifies, the trumpets (II). The start of the combat drama comes third because the three antagonists (dragon, beast, false prophet) mimic the divine Trinity. Their overthrow is sixth, even as humanity came along on the sixth day of the creation week (Gen 1), to emphasize the beast's humanity and to polemicize against the deification of humans in Greco-Roman ruler cults. Seventh is the new Jerusalem, the perfect outcome of God's purpose.

9. Yarbro Collins recognizes the literary device that links one section to another by introducing motifs from a subsequent section toward the end of the section that precedes it (1- . . . -1-2-1 / 2- . . . -2-3-2 / 3- . . . -3, etc.). She calls it "interlocking," and considers it a key to the structure. Collins, *Combat Myth*, 16–19. Bruce W. Longenecker calls it a chain link, based on a reference in Lucian (ἄλυσις [*halysis*]). "Linked Like a Chain," esp. 112–13. Longenecker finds a reference to the same device in Quintillian.

expectation of the battle of Armageddon (16:16), which does not happen until 19:17–21; and three verses after mention of Armageddon, "God remembered great Babylon" (16:19) points toward the judgment of Babylon that succeeds immediately (17—19:10). Toward the end of the judgment on Babylon we hear of a messianic wedding (19:7–9)—as also in 21:2 toward the end of the next subsection—which comes about at 21:9ff. These clasps, as minor foreshadowings, indicate the continuity of the string of visions.

Foreshadowing on a larger scale explains the patches of material that remain unaccounted for, namely the vision of the protection and final bliss of God's people (chapter 7), the "little scroll" passage (10:1—11:13), and the triple announcement of God's judgment (14:6–13). Let us examine each of these in turn.

Chapter 7 falls toward the end of the first series of seven, between the sixth and seventh seals. It focuses on the people of God, sealed for protection against the impending trumpets (7:1–8; cf. 9:4), and delivered from the great tribulation into everlasting peace (7:9–17). Thus the saints are set over against the masses who must flee the wrath of God and of the Lamb (cf. 6:15–17). In the first part, the prominent number 144,000 is introduced (cf. 14:1–5, 21:16–17). The concluding poem (7:15–17), with its description of the bliss of the redeemed, looks ahead to 20:6 and 21:3–4. By placing these previews of the happiness of God's people here near the beginning, the writer offsets the gloom of the seals, trumpets, bowls, and Babylon material with a ray of hope; he sketches in advance the divine response to the martyrs' cry for redress (cf. 6:9–11); and he creates an inclusio spanning and uniting chapters 6–22 (sections I to VII).

In chapter 10 an angel, after swearing that the seventh trumpet will signal the fulfillment of all prophecy (10:5–7), makes John eat a little scroll and tells him he must prophesy again (10:8–11), which he begins to do immediately (11:1–13) before the seventh trumpet is blown (11:14–19). The new prophecy, with its three-and-a-half-years (11:2, 3) and its story about a beast making war on prophet-martyrs whom God vindicates by resurrection (11:4–13), is a synopsis of the later combat scenarios (12–15; 19–20).[10] At face value this creates a second inclusio, concentric within the larger inclusio of 6–22, enclosing everything from the trumpets to the close of the second panel of combat material (8:6—21:8; sections II to VI).

If the foreshadowing in chapter 7 ties together visions I and VII, and the same technique in 10:1—11:13 relates visions II and VI, we might expect the middle of chapter 14, just before the first act of the war drama closes (14:14—15:4), to unite visions III and V. Instead 14:6–13 points ahead to all four following visions. Three angels streak across the sky proclaiming the hour of God's judgment: on the world (14:6–7), on Babylon the great (14:8), and on the kingdom of the beast (14:9–11), followed by words for the saints (14:12–13). This is a programmatic statement to help the reader sort out what follows.[11]

---

10. Yarbro Collins is right to take the little scroll of chapter 10 as a pointer to the combat drama in 12–15, 19–20, though she does not make a point of the thematic unity of 11:1–13 with this material. Collins, *Combat Myth*, 19–32. Mark Seaborn Hall also recognizes 10:11—11:1 as marking a division, though he tries in vain to make it the organizing principle of the book. See "Hook Interlocking Structure." These interpretations of the little scroll as a second prophecy are more convincing than Richard Bauckham's attempt to make it out to be identical with the seven-sealed scroll of chapter 5. Bauckham, *Climax*, 243–57.

11. Like the heavenly flight and triple "Woe" of the eagle in 8:13, the flights of the three angels in 14:6–11 are a meta-revelation to explain the revelations that follow. These textual markers do not advance the narrative as such.

Hour of God's judgment	Visionary representation
On the world (14:6–7)	Bowls (15:5—16:21)
On Babylon (14:8)	Judgment of Babylon (17:1—19:10)
On kingdom of beast (14:9–11)	Combat resolved (19:11—21:8)
Concerning saints (14:12–13)	Glory of Jerusalem (21:9—22:9)

Positioned where it is toward the midst of chapters 6–22, the programmatic 14:6–13 divides the visions into a group of three that move the narrative up to the hour of judgment (seals, trumpets, combat joined), followed by a group of four that focus on various aspects of the hour of judgment itself (bowls, Babylon, combat resolved, Jerusalem). Formally, each of the first three visions contains an expansion that foreshadows what will be shown later, whereas the last four follow one another directly.

Large scroll of chap. 5	Little scroll of chap. 10
Seven seals (6 + 8:1, 3–5)	
Preview of outcome for saints: chap. 7	
Seven trumpets (8:2 + 8:6—9:21 + 11:14–19)	
	Preview of outcome of little scroll: 11:1–13
	Combat joined (12:1—14:5; 14:14–20; 15:2–4)
Synopsis of four visions to follow: 14:6–13	
Seven bowls (15:1 + 15:5—16:21)	
Judgment of Babylon (17—19:10)	
	Combat resolved (19:11—21:8)
Glory of Jerusalem (21:9—22:9)	

In sum, the seven symbolic visions of chapters 6–22 interweave two quite different stories of the last things. Based on their internal matter, they divide into one group of three-plus-two, and another of two. The five framing visions admonish corrupted churches not to take part in a society under death-warrant, while the combat drama (12–15; 19–20) provides special encouragement for suffering churches such as Smyrna and Philadelphia. Thus chapters 6–22 correspond broadly to the seven epistolary oracles of chapters 2–3.

SECONDARY LEVEL OF ORGANIZATION

At a more detailed level of organization, John uses similar devices to guide his reader.

The seals, the trumpets, and the bowls, for example, are each divided themselves into groups of four and of three units. In the early seals, the four living creatures of the heavenly throne-room (cf. 4:6–7) invite John to "Come," and four riders on horses of different colors appear (6:1–8),[12] while the remaining three seal-units are freer in wording and somewhat longer (6:9–11; 6:12–17; 8:1, 3–5).

When the first four trumpets are blown, natural elements—hail and fire, a burning mountain, a falling star, and the sun—each destroy "a third" of something in the physical world (8:6–12). In 8:13, an eagle announces three woes to come. Again the remaining three trumpets are much more expansive. Each is circumscribed, not only by counting the blasts as they

12. Since the horse-and-rider seals form a group, the rider on the white horse (6:2), like the other three riders, represents a human blight, in this case wars on earth before the Parousia. It has nothing to do with Christ (cf. 19:11), as is so frequently asserted on arbitrary grounds. De Villiers, "Role of Composition." This clear example illustrates the importance of doing structural analysis before jumping to a conclusion about the significance of a symbol in the Apocalypse.

occur (9:1, 13; 11:15), but also by references to the woes in retrospect (9:12; 11:14).

Poetic exclamations by angels after the first three bowls (16:5–7) punctuate the hebdomad of chapter 16. Here the order of four plus three, used earlier in the seals and the trumpets, is reversed to three plus four, making the numerical scheme of this, the first of the "hour of God's judgment" visions (15:5—22:9), correspond to that of the epistolary oracles (three oracles: 2:1–17 / four: 2:18—3:22) and of the symbolic visions of chapters 6–22 (three visions: 6:1—15:4 / four: 15:5—22:9).

LINEAR PROGRESS / RECAPITULATIONS

Having observed the main structural divisions, we return to the question about narrative progress. Do chapters 6–22 proceed in an uninterrupted line, or do they repeat the same story several times over?

This is a question of content as well as of form. To answer it we have to determine the basic reference of a few of the visions. It seems plain enough that the very end of the world is depicted at the close of each of the seven subsections.

Cosmic dissolution; fire cast upon the earth	6:12–17 + 8:1–5
Kingdom of the world has become the kingdom of God and of his Christ	11:15–19
Reaping of the earth; winepress of God's wrath; hymn of the conquerors	14:14—15:4
"It is done!"; totalitarian earthquake	16:17–21
Babylon fallen, followed by marriage supper of the Lamb	19:1–10
New heaven and new earth	21:1–8
God shines for ever on new Jerusalem	22:1–5

The end is foreshadowed in other passages too (e.g., 7:15–17; 17:14, 16–17), making at least nine scenes of consummation. Some of these accent the dissolution of the world at the end of the present age (6:12–17 + 8:5; 14:14–20; 16:17–21), others the extension of God's rule over his creation (e.g., 11:15–19; 17:14, 16–17; 19:1–9), yet others the nature of the final, eternal state of things (e.g., 7:15–17; 21:1–8; 21:9—22:5). Therefore the seven symbolic visions, with their related material, all reach more or less the same goal. They are recurrent with respect to their common terminus.[13]

Recapitulation on a larger literary scale is suggested by the device of two revelatory scrolls (chap. 5; chap. 10), and by the directive, "You must again prophesy" (10:11).

Yet there are also indications of plot development.[14] Divine pressure on the human race to repent intensifies from the seals to the trumpets to the bowls. The social and economic woes of the first four seals (6:1–8) are natural, in contrast to the plagues that wipe out "thirds" of geographical features (8:7–12) and the demonically inspired wars of multitudes (chap. 9); the bowls, as "the last" in which the wrath of God is expended (15:1) deface everything without exception (16:2–10, 17, 20). An early vision of the martyrs waiting to be vindicated and avenged (6:9–11) finds its answer later (foreshadowed at 7:15–17; 11:11–13; 11:18; 15:2–4; 16:4–6; 18:20; 19:2; fulfilled at 20:4–6). The sealing of the 144,000 on their foreheads (7:1–8) protects them from the trumpets (9:4) and the bowls (16:2, 10). Chapters 6–14 move toward the "hour of God's judgment" heralded

13. Collins, *Combat Myth*, 32–44.

14. Jauhiainen, "Recapitulation and Progression." Jauhiainen finds more progression than many recent commentators do. In the article cited he does not consider the view, which I regard as virtually certain, that the series of heptads (seals, trumpets, and bowls) commence progressively but terminate at the same point.

at 14:6–11 and carried out in chapters 15–20. A global mobilization to Armageddon (16:14) leads to the fateful conflict (19:11–21). Jerusalem shines in majesty (21:9—22:9) after the downfall of all her enemies.

Hence the story-line of chapters 6–22 has momentum toward the finale, but allows for reiteration within the subsections, focusing especially on aspects of the end.

SUMMARY

Between the prescript and the postscript, the body of the book of Revelation consists of two main sections: seven oracles of Christ (chaps. 1–3), followed by seven symbolic visions given by God through the Lamb (chaps. 4–22). These main sections are alike subdivided into twos and fives, threes and fours, and so correspond to each other in their use of formal devices as well as in tenor. Through this duple vehicle John calls the church to forsake a world-system careening toward damnation and to persevere in the way of righteousness that leads through testing to ultimate glory. His summons, issued first in prophetic prose for the sake of relative clarity (1–3), is reinforced by the apocalyptic narrative of chapters 4–22 for the sake of motivational effect.

4

Cracking the Code

THAT THE language of the Apocalypse is richly figurative is recognized by all. The book wears this feature on its face. Even dispensationalists, who aim to interpret prophecy literally, recognize that the Lamb is Christ, the dragon is Satan, the beast represents a human ruler, and so on. Not whether the book uses symbols, but how extensively, and in reference to what, are the issues.

Figurative language is notoriously ambiguous. Symbolism involves comparing one thing with another, usually to bring out a sole point they have in common. When the point is correctly grasped, the advantage of using the symbol is that it enhances vividness and rhetorical effect.[1] But there is always a risk that hearers will take the comparison in a sense other than intended. In the Revelation, Christ is presented as a lamb because he gave his life on the cross in fulfillment of the Israelite sacrificial cultus, not because he will crush the beast with his horns.[2] The possibility of misunderstanding shadows all symbolic language,

---

1. John used symbols "so that we should actually see and perceive spiritual reality and not merely listen to abstractions about it, and accordingly be shocked." Beale, "Purpose of Symbolism in Revelation," 65.

2. On Christ as the Lamb in the Revelation, see Aune, *Revelation*, 1.367–73; Hofius, "Ἀρνίον—Lamm." The evidence for the use of lambs or sheep as symbols of rulers in biblical or Jewish literature is sparse in comparison with sacrificial associations.

whether the comparison be explicit in a simile ("a loud voice *like* a trumpet" 1:10), or implicit in a metaphor, which superimposes a secondary image on the reality ("the Lion . . . has conquered" 5:5).[3]

Thankfully, the Apocalypse is peppered with clues to its own code. Not every symbol is explained, but all the chief ones are, enough to unlock the message beyond reasonable doubt. While those interpreters who champion a literal approach do so with the commendable aim of submitting their imagination to the authority of the sacred page, the best way to avoid rampant speculation is to follow the pointers embedded in the text, interpreting them against the book's cultural setting. These should be our foundation, not pre-judgments about preterism, historicism, futurism, or idealism, much less about how to harmonize supposed information about the last things in the Revelation with that found in Daniel or other parts of the Old Testament. We can bypass a good deal of unprofitable theoretical debate about the proper hermeneutical approach to the Revelation by letting the book itself instruct us.

KEYS TO THE SYMBOLS

Scattered throughout the book are several kinds of clues to the symbols: explicit declarations, interpretive glosses, deliberate logical incompatibilities, use of numerology, and free allusions to scripture.

1. Declarations

Sometimes John states outright that the language is figurative. In the superscription, he says God gave him the revelation "to show (δεῖξαι [*deixai*]) to his servants," and that he "signified

3. On simile and metaphor in the Bible, see Caird, *Language and Imagery of the Bible*, 144–59.

(ἐσήμανεν [*esēmanen*) it" (1:1). Neither verb is restricted to ordinary prose, and the latter indicates the use of signs to get across a meaning. Standing where it does at the head, this statement applies to the book as a whole.[4]

To set the tone, the very first vision (1:12–16) is called a "mystery (μυστήριον [*mystērion*], 1:20)," a mystical figure. An allegorical explanation of two of its elements is given: the stars signify tutelary angels, and the lampstands their churches.

Mention is made at 11:8 of a great city named Sodom, Egypt, and the place where Jesus was crucified. The names are to be understood "spiritually (πνευματικῶς [*pneumatikōs*])," indicating that their sense is other than geographical.

Later the harlot bears on her forehead the name "Babylon the Great," which is also said to be a "mystery" or cryptogram (17:5). Israel remembered historic Babylon for its arrogance toward the God of Israel and its ruthlessness in carrying off the people into captivity (cf. Isa 13–14), and these qualities exist in the harlot as well (17:6; 18:7).[5] That both the cities in 11:8 and 17:5 have the epithet "the great" identifies them as "the great city which has dominion over the kings of the earth" (17:18), which was, at the time of writing, Rome, empress of the Mediterranean.[6]

Some rich images are styled "signs (σημεῖα [*sēmeia*])." These include the celestial woman (12:1–2), the dragon (12:3–4), and the plagues of the bowls (15:1). Let us take up each in turn. The woman, adorned with the sun, the moon, and twelve stars—a constellation found elsewhere in scripture only in reference to Jacob, Rachel and the patriarchs of Israel (Gen 37:9–10)—gives birth to Jesus (Rev 12:4–6), and is the mother of those who bear

4. Beale, "Purpose of Symbolism in Revelation," 54–55.

5. Sals, *Biographie "Babylon."*

6. Biguzzi, "Babylon in Revelation."

testimony to Jesus (12:17). Her escape from the dragon, like the former deliverance of Israel from Egypt, comes through flight into the wilderness on an eagle's wings (Exod 19:4). Putting together these associations, she represents the people of God corporate, Mother Zion, the church in continuity with believing Israel of old.[7]

An interpretation of the dragon is laid down in 12:9 (cf. 20:2): he is "that ancient serpent, who is called the devil and Satan." This alludes to the snake in the primeval temptation account (Gen 3:1–15). His red color (Rev 12:3) and his casting down a third of the stars with his tail (12:4) denote a violent, deadly nature opposed to the order of God's creation. Around this central identity gather a number of related characteristics. His power to stir up the waves of the sea (12:17—13:5) is a feature he has absorbed from the chaos monster of Near Eastern mythology, adapted into the Old Testament as Leviathan (Isa 27:1; cf. Job 41; Psa 104:26) or Rahab (Job 26:12; Psa 89:10). Also shared with Rahab and Leviathan is his role as the pursuer at the exodus (Rev 12:13–16), derived from the Old Testament (Psa 74:13–14; Isa 30:7; 51:9–10). His seven heads (Rev 12:3) align him with the polycephalous Leviathan (Psa 74:13–14; cf. Lotan in the Ugaritic epic: *ANET*, p. 138, g. I* AB, [i]), and the ten horns with Daniel's fourth beast from the sea (Dan 7:7, 20, 24).[8]

If the seven bowl-plagues are a "sign" (Rev 15:1), then they are something other than a screenplay of exactly what will take place in the future. Sores on people, water turning to blood,

---

7. Riley, "Woman Rev 12?" Almost no commentators beyond Roman Catholic circles imagine the woman of chapter 12 to be Mary pictured as the queen of heaven, as we still find in Grelot, "Mére." For a collection of some 28 different identifications of the woman, see Buby, "Fascinating Woman of Rev 12."

8. Further on the dragon: Bauckham, *Climax of Prophecy*, 185–98; Busch, *Gefallene Drache*.

impenetrable darkness, and hail (16:2, 3–4, 10, 21) recall the plagues against Egypt that preceded the exodus (Exod 7:14–24; 9:8–12, 22–35; 10:21–29). John taps the known form of past plagues to indicate typologically the signs, of whatever sort, that will portend God's intervention at the end of the world (cf. Luke 21:25–26). Since the plagues of the trumpets (Rev 8–9) run closely parallel to those of the bowls (Rev 16), the trumpet-visions too are "signs" using types from the past, for example the locusts (9:1–11; cf. Exod 10:12–20), and do not provide a documentary before the fact. Because of their Old Testament background, chapters 8–9 and 16 ring with overtones of God's just wrath against a society that has tempted and roughly handled his beloved ones, and of his mighty moving to deliver them.

In two places, the reader is invited to use "wisdom (σοφία [*sophia*])" and "understanding (νοῦς [*nous*])" to interpret figures, namely, the number of the beast (Rev 13:18) and the details concerning the beast and the harlot (17:9). This should tip off the reader that the number 666 goes deeper than arithmetic calculations. All attempts to find the name of an actual ruler, whether in Greco-Roman antiquity or in the political scene of the modern interpreter, the numerical values of whose letters add up to 666, have failed.[9] Instead, the number has numerological significance. It is a triple, therefore emphatic, asseveration that the beast falls short of the perfection ("seven") that is falsely claimed for him as an object of worship in rivalry to the one God (cf. 13:12–15). As the human race was created on day

---

9. *Pace* the ingenious exercises focusing on the emperor Nero in Bauckham, *Climax of Prophecy*, 384–407. Bauckham has done about as much as can be done to exhaust the possibilities of alphanumeric manipulation. Aune seems to favor a more symbolic interpretation: *Revelation*, 2.773–75. For a confirming judgment that calculations have been unsuccessful, see Marucci, "Gematrie."

six of the creation week (Gen 1:26–31), so the beast, in spite of his vaunted divinity, is in fact human, human, human.

So also every venture of commentators to match the seven (eight) kings of Rev 17:10–11 with any given set of Roman emperors has come to shipwreck on the facts of history, which yield too many emperors before Domitian.[10] The seven heads of the beast represent the "completion" of the number of kings of the earth down through history, the grand sum of governments insofar as they have ranged themselves against God and his purposes. In the 90s A.D. John had the imperium of Rome especially in view. Just as John's beast amalgamates into a composite figure (Rev 13:2) empires that Daniel saw as a succession (Dan 7:1–8), so the number seven presents the reigning Roman emperor as the culmination of all who went before him.

2. Glosses

Explanatory remarks along the way offer another key to the symbols, usually in the formula "A is B," where A is the symbol and B its referent (1:20; 4:5; 5:6, 8; 7:13–14; 11:3–4; 14:3–4; 16:13–14; 17:9–12, 15, 18; 19:8; 20:5).[11] Often the angel who is showing the visions offers a commentary. Sometimes the author himself inserts a gloss.

"The seven stars *are* the angels of the seven churches . . . The seven lampstands *are* the seven churches" (1:20). With this information in hand, we can surmise that the star fallen to earth who opens the shaft of the abyss (9:1) is also an angel (cf. 20:1); and that the two lampstands in a difficult verse (11:4) represent the church. Torches before the throne in heaven, and the seven

10. Aune, *Revelation*, 3.947–48.

11. Michaels, "Revelation 1.19," 608–17. Covering several of the same passages, but somewhat clogged with methodology, is Lee, *Narrative Asides*.

eyes of the Lamb, "are" the spirits of God (4:5; 5:6). Golden bowls full of incense "are" prayers of the saints ascending into God's presence (5:8). An innumerable multitude in white robes, with palm branches in their hands, "are" those who come out of the great tribulation unspotted (7:13–14). Fine linen "is" the righteous deeds of the saints (19:8), and again we can use this to pin down the meaning of white garments in other places (3:4–5, 18; 4:4; 6:11; 7:9, 13–14; 15:6; 19:14).[12] The 144,000 purchased out of the earth who have not defiled themselves with women are, by apposition, those redeemed from the earth: they "are" the followers of the Lamb who spurn the beast, first fruits to God (14:3–4)—in other words, believers (cf. "first fruits" at Rom 8:23; Jas 1:18).

In a very dense passage, two witnesses "are" olive trees and "are" lampstands (11:3–4). Here is an allusion to Zechariah 4:11–14, itself opaque. In the post-exilic context of Zechariah 3–4, the "two anointed" are Joshua the high priest and Zerubbabel, the royal descendant appointed local governor, both empowered by the Holy Spirit to rebuild the temple and its community, represented by a seven-bowled pedestal lamp receiving oil. Since we already know lampstands mean churches (1:20), and given the fact that John consistently emphasizes the priestly and royal properties of the church (Rev 1:6; 7:15; 20:6), the echoes of Joshua and Zerubbabel in 11:4 make concrete these dual aspects of his ecclesiology.

An important set of identifications is given in John's exchange with the revealing angel in 17:7–18, focusing on the big characters of the beast and the harlot. The seven heads of the beast are polysemous: they "are" the seven fabled hills of Rome (v. 9), but they "are" also the totality of the imperial succession, as heirs to all former empires (v. 10). One member, after suf-

---

12. McIlraith, "Fine Linen."

fering a blow and disappearing from the scene, "is" an eighth who will return for another incumbency (v. 11; cf. 13:3).[13] Ten, like seven, denotes completeness; the ten horns "are" leaders of all the nations of the world, who will be confederate with the beast in his final manifestation (vv. 12–14). Many waters "are" peoples and multitudes and nations and tongues (v. 15), and the harlot "is" Roman commercial society in its immense attractiveness to the lands conquered by her armies (v. 18).[14] The glosses in chapter 17 are keys to a correct interpretation of the beasts in chapter 13.

Frogs out of the mouths of dragon, beast, and false prophet "are" deceptive demons (16:13–14). The dragon finds his own interpretation in 20:3, where it is reiterated that he "is" the devil and Satan (cf. 12:9).

In 20:4 John recounts a vision of martyrs coming to life to reign with Christ, then adds that this resurrection "is the first" (v. 5). As another instance of the formula "A is B," this too is an interpretive gloss: the resurrection of verse 4 symbolizes something that needs to be spelled out in this aside. What it represents is the exact contrary, both verbal and substantive, of the "second death" (20:6). If the second death is the irreversible death-state of an impenitent individual in the age to come (the lake of fire, 20:14) consequent upon death in the present age, the

---

13. Strictly the Greek of 17:11 does not say this "eighth" is "*one* of the seven," as it is often translated on the assumption that the author is tapping the myth, crystallizing in his day, of Nero revived. The genitive construction could just as naturally qualify the resurgent beast as "part and parcel of," or "belonging to" the seven, the "eighth" being the essence behind its "seven" embodiments in various human governments throughout history.

14. Bauckham, "The Economic Critique of Rome in Revelation 18," in *Climax*, 338–83; Royalty, *Streets of Heaven*; Callahan, "Apocalypse as Critique Rev 18."

first resurrection is the entrance of a Christian martyr into inalienable immortality during the present age as the first phase toward the full experience of permanent life in the age to come.[15]

3. Deliberate Logical Incompatibilities

In quite a number of places, the Apocalypse juxtaposes images that do not fit together logically. This is another indication that the language is symbolic.

Within two verses the Son of God is presented under the mixed metaphors of a lion, a root, and a lamb (5:5–6). All allude to passages of the Old Testament (lion: Gen 49:9–10; root: a conjunction of Isa 4:2 + 11:1 + 53:2; lamb: Isa 53:7).

To plunge cloth into blood would stain it red, not launder it white (7:14). But the death of Jesus cleanses a human life of guilt for wrong acts.

A temple is not two witnesses (11:1–3), witnesses are not olive trees, nor are olive trees lampstands (11:4), although Joshua the high priest and Zerubbabel the governor were at one time two anointed ones serving the Israelite temple (Zech 4:11–14 in context). Nor were Jeremiah whose words were a fire (Jer 5:14), Elijah whose prayer brought on a drought (1 Kings 17:1), and Moses who smote the earth with plagues (Exod 7–12) identical, though their outstanding achievements blend in the two witnesses of Revelation 11 (vv. 5–6). Revelation 11:3–6 cannot be understood except as a heap of Old Testament allusions freely adapted to describe the temple of God, now the church (3:12; 7:15; 21:22 with 21:3), as a royal entity with a priestly role and prophetic gifts.

Sodom, Egypt, and Jerusalem were different places, yet they all denominate a single "city" (11:8). "Sodom": the people of this city are "wicked, great sinners against the LORD" (Gen

15. Kline, "First Resurrection."

13:13); "Egypt": they "deal shrewdly" with God's people and "oppress" them (Exod 1:10, 12); Jesus' crucifixion near Jerusalem: this city will persecute his followers to the death, as in fact happens in the immediate context (Rev 11:7–10). As we saw above, the reference is to the civilization of the world, centered in Rome (cf. 17:18).

Dragon and beast alike have seven heads and ten horns (12:3; 13:1), numbers and images that do not tally. By setting side by side the prime number seven and the number ten, of which seven is no factor, the author discourages the reader from trying to picture the horns distributed somehow on the heads. Each number has its own independent, symbolic significance, as we saw above.

A bride is not a city (21:9–10). They are two complementary symbols of a particular human community, the body of the redeemed.

Wherever in the Apocalypse images do not jive though referring to the same entity, we know they are figures.

4. Numerology

Most of the numbers in the Revelation have symbolic value and are not quantitative.[16]

Why, if the witnesses represent the church, are there "two" of them (11:3–4, 10)? While duality may be suggested by the "two anointed" of the background text (Zech 4:11–14), these witnesses speak God's final warning to an unreceptive world. The doubling of a matter from God indicates its fixity and urgency (cf. Gen 41:32), and two witnesses are needed to establish a capital charge (Num 35:30; Deut 17:6; 19:15).

---

16. On the use of particular numbers in the New Testament (two, three, four, etc.), see Schmitz, Hemer, Harris, and Brown, "Number," *NIDNTT* 2.683–704.

The trio of the dragon, the beast, and the false prophet (16:13) is a parody of the Trinity: the Almighty, the King of kings, and the Spirit who imbues the prophetic church.

Three-and-a-half years (Rev 11:2–3; 12:6, 14; 13:5) is a figure that comes from the book of Daniel, where it denoted the period (168–164 B.C.) during which Antiochus Epiphanes IV practiced outrages upon Jerusalem, desecrated the temple and persecuted the faithful in Israel (Dan 7:25; 8:14; 9:27; 12:11; cf. 1 Macc 1:29–30, 41, 54; 4:52–54). In the Revelation it has become a cipher for a time of stress for God's people, limited by the divine counsel.

Four comprises the corners of a square, and so represents the total surface of the earth (7:1–2; 20:8). The four living creatures nearest the heavenly throne have as their domain the creation, as is evident in any case from their special characteristics drawn from wild and domestic animals, humankind, and birds (4:7).

Six, as we saw, was the day in the creation week on which God made human beings (Gen 1) and falls short of divine perfection by one, so emphasizes the humanity of the beastly emperor whom a foolish world honors as divine (13:18).

Seven is the most prominent number, used many times throughout the book. It represents fullness, perfection, maturation.[17] Oracles addressed to seven churches (chaps. 2–3) are for the church catholic. Seven seals, seven trumpets, seven bowls—each connotes the ripening of God's judgment upon a degraded world. The Lamb's seven horns (5:6) symbolize his plenitude of power. Seven spirits of God (1:4; 5:6) represent the abundant potencies of the Holy Spirit (cf. Isa 11:2; Zech 4:2, 6, 10b).

Ten, the number of the fingers on both hands, points to universality. Ten horns signify all the kings of the world, who will form an alliance with the beast (Rev 17:12–13). But "ten

---

17. Aune, *Revelation*, 1.114–15.

days" (2:10) heartens the imprisoned that their tribulation will be short (cf. 12:12; 17:10; 20:3).

Twelve, as the number of the tribes of Israel (7:5–8; 21:12, 19–20; cf. Gen 37:9–10; Rev 12:1) and of the apostles of the Lamb (21:14), connotes the people of God. Patriarchs and apostles can be combined to demonstrate the continuity of faithful Israel and the church (Exod 19:6 with Rev 1:6; cf. 1 Pet 2:9), either by addition to make twenty-four (4:4, 10, etc.), or by multiplication to make a hundred and forty-four (21:17; cf. 7:4; 14:1, 3).

Integers may be squared or cubed to intensify their significance. "One thousand six hundred stadia" (14:20), the distance that blood will flow from Jerusalem when God treads his winepress, is the square of four multiplied by the square of ten. Since four and ten each symbolize completeness, their squares multiplied together represent God's judgment as comprehensive.

Because the inner sanctum of Solomon's temple had been a perfect cube (1 Kings 6:20), the use of cubic numbers in the Revelation signifies that which is consecrated to God. This is certainly the case with the dimensions of the new Jerusalem, which forms a cube with sides of twelve thousand stadia in length (Rev 21:16). No physical city is cubical, nor would it be practical to build one of proportions equivalent to 1500 miles. John relies on the common sense and the biblical sense of his readers. A thousand is the cube of ten; this is multiplied by the number of God's people. Hence the mathematics underscore the idea of the community of the redeemed (12) as God's final sanctuary ($10 \times 10 \times 10$) in the new creation ("he will dwell with them," 20:3). In the same way, the 144,000 (7:4; 14:1, 3) are the elect comprising the Church Universal, the total body of Old and New Testament believers (12×12), whom God has sanctified to be his final dwelling place on earth (10 × 10 × 10).[18] The thousand years (20:2–7) are the final epoch of the present age that God sanctifies (cube of ten, cf. "hallowed," Gen 2:3) to be a world sabbath rest for formerly mistreated witnesses.[19]

5. *Free Allusions To The Old Testament*

John draws from the Old Testament, and expects a biblically literate reader to pick up on resonances. Indeed, a majority of the material in the Revelation originates in the Hebrew scriptures, but John reworks it for a new setting. The result is a curious patchwork of old matter in fresh relationships. That there are no actual quotes in the welter of allusions is due to the fact that the author is not so much appealing to an authoritative text (though it is his authority), as quarrying it for evocative prototypes.[20] This is not the place to produce an encyclopedia of scriptural echoes in the Apocalypse, which would require a technical commentary on the whole book.[21] But it may be illuminating to highlight a few of the more salient complexes of Old Testament material.

Even as God led Israel out of bondage in Egypt and on toward the promised land (Exod 1–24), so a greater exodus is about to liberate the church from this world and conduct her into God's kingdom. The historic plagues against Pharaoh serve as types for the trumpets and the bowls (Exod 7–12; cf. Rev 8–9, 16). Pharaoh chased Israel to the Red Sea; in the same way the dragon will pursue the celestial woman (Exod 14; cf. Rev

18. Beale, *Revelation*, 416–23.

19. Kellerman, "Why One Thousand?"

20. Moyise, *OT in Revelation*; "OT in NT"; Decock, "Scriptures in Revelation"; Glonner, *Bildersprache*; Moyise, "Does Author of Revelation Misappropriate?"; "Intertextuality in Revelation."

21. See Beale, *Revelation*. Beale is so thorough in this regard that he often explores minutiae of questionable significance.

12:13–16).²² But the account of Pharaoh's army being engulfed in the waters of the Red Sea is transmuted into a different story: the dragon pours a flood out of his mouth to sweep the woman away, which the earth quaffs to help her (cf. Rev 12:15–16). There follows a hymn of victory (Exod 15; cf. Rev 15:2–4).²³ Israel pitched camp in the wilderness (Exod 16–19); so also there is a camp of the saints (Rev 20:9), with a census carefully taken (Num 1–4, 26; cf. Rev 7:4–8).

Moses made the tabernacle according to a heavenly pattern (Exod 25:9, 40; 26:30; 31:11; Num 8:4). John reverses the direction of thought and projects the plan of the earthly temple into heaven. While there above, he sees a temple (Rev 11:19; 14:15, 17; 15:5–8; 16:1, 17) stocked with all the necessary furniture. The laver or "sea" of molten bronze (Exod 30:17–21; 1 Kings 7:23–26) gives place to one made of glass like crystal (Rev 4:6; 15:2).²⁴ There is an altar of blood sacrifice (Exod 27:1–8; cf. Rev 6:9; 11:1; 14:18; 16:7); a golden altar of incense (Exod 30:1–10; cf. Rev 5:8; 8:3–5; 9:13); and the ark of the covenant (Exod 25:10–22; cf. Rev 11:19). Instead of priests and Levites, the attendants of the heavenly temple are angels (Rev 5:8; 8:3–5; 14:15, 17–18; 15:5–8).²⁵

From Isaiah, John has learned of the seraphim surrounding the divine throne (Isa 6:2–3; cf. Rev 4:8); how the sky gives way when God comes to eclipse an empire (Isa 13:10; 34:4; cf. Rev 6:12–17); and how to raise a taunt over fallen Babylon (Isa 13–14; 21:9; 47; cf. Rev 14:8; 18:2ff.). Isaiah also supplies glimpses of

22. Dochhorn, "Erde tat Mund auf, Apc 12,16."

23. Moyise, "Singing the Song of Moses."

24. Options for understanding the puzzling "sea of glass" are reviewed in Böttrich, "Gläserne Meer."

25. On the theme of the temple in John's Apocalypse, see Briggs, *Jewish Temple Imagery in Revelation*; Stevenson, *Temple and Identity*; Ben-Daniel and Ben Daniel, *Apocalypse in Light of Temple*.

Jerusalem in her future glory (Isa 60; cf. Rev 21:10—22:5), and of a new heaven and a new earth (Isa 65:17–25; cf. Rev 21).

Ezekiel saw the appearance of the likeness of the glory of the LORD sitting on a throne, surrounded by cherubim, as did John (Ezek 1; cf. Rev 4:2, 6–9). Both prophets received God's word by eating a visionary scroll (Ezek 3:1–3; cf. Rev 10:8–11). In Ezekiel the righteous ones among the people receive a protective seal on their foreheads, probably in the form of a letter "t" or a cross, before God executes judgment on the rest (Ezek 9; cf. Rev 7:1–4).[26] Ezekiel knows of a resurrection of sorts (Ezek 37; cf. Rev 20:4–6) followed by a last attack on Israel by the nations led by Gog of the land of Magog (Ezek 38–39; cf. Rev 19:17–21; 20:7–10). He is invited to observe an angel measuring the restored temple (Ezek 40–44; cf. Rev 21:15–17), though John is told to perform a similar measurement himself (Rev 11:1–2). Whereas Ezekiel, a priest of that covenant which shadowed forth things to come, pictures the eternal resting place of God on earth (Ezek 43:7) as an idealized temple with an updated edition of the Torah for its constitution (Ezek 40–48), John contemplates an eternity without any sacred edifice, where the unmediated presence of God himself with his people has superseded any temple (Rev 21:22). Both seers are granted a vision of the river of life and of the tree of life (Ezek 47:1–12; cf. Rev 22:1–2).

Daniel describes a series of regimes over the saints culminating in a monstrous beast (Dan 7:1–7; cf. Rev 13:2, 5–7) having ten horns (Dan 7:7, 20, 24; cf. Rev 13:1; 17:3, 7, 12–14). Already in Daniel's day Nebuchadnezzar had an image made to be worshipped (Dan 3; cf. Rev 13:14–15). The beast is deposed when one like a son of man receives the kingdom from God (Dan 7:9–13; cf. Rev 5; 14:14). Nevertheless, Daniel predicts

26. Beale, *Revelation*, 410.

a period of tribulation for the faithful lasting three-and-a-half years (Dan 7:25; 8:14; 9:27; 12:11; cf. Rev 11:2–3; 12:6, 14; 13:5), during which Michael the archangel will stand up and fight on their behalf (Dan 12:1; cf. Rev 12:7–9).

The prophet Joel foresaw a plague of locusts having the appearance of horses (Joel 2:4; cf. Rev 9:7), and spoke of an eschatological mobilization of all nations against Israel (Joel 3:1–16; cf. Rev 9:7–11, 16–19; 11:7; 13:7; 16:13–16; 19:11–21; 20:7–10). In response, God will reap the earth (Joel 3:13; cf. Rev 14:14–20).[27]

Zechariah records visions involving four riders on horses going out through all the earth (Zech 1:7–17; 6:1–8; Rev 6:1–8); two olive trees (Zech 4; cf. Rev 11:4); and a description of a ritually purified and holy Jerusalem (Zech 14; cf. Rev 21:22—22:5).

Although these images and many others from the Old Testament inform the book of Revelation, all of them are malleable in John's hands. The interpreter must be as sensitive in noting subtle nuances introduced by John, as John, under prophetic inspiration, is flexible in his manipulation of the raw data.

The five keys to the symbolism of the Apocalypse we have just reviewed form categories of passages that overlap and reinforce one another. Controversy about what our basic hermeneutical stance ought to be is forestalled by the fact that one of the things the book teaches is how to interpret itself. On the basis of its own explicit indications, we conclude that John's use of figurative language in virtually every chapter is lavish. Whether we consider the accoutrements of the living Christ (chap. 1), or the

---

27. The harvest of Revelation 14:14–16 represents divine retribution on the nations, in development of Joel 3:13 and in parallelism with Revelation 14:17–20. Against the view that the harvest is an image of redemption, see Beale, *Revelation*, 770–78; Mathewson, "Destiny of the Nations"; Herms, *Apocalypse for Church and World*.

heavenly throne scene (chapters 4–5), whether the seals, trumpets, and bowls (chaps. 6, 8–9, 11, 15–16), or the 144,000 (chaps. 7, 14), or the two witnesses (chap. 11), or the names of cities (chaps. 11, 17, 21), or the antithetical women (chaps. 12, 17, 21), or the dragon and the beasts (chaps. 12–13, 17), or the harvest of the earth (chap. 14), or the harlot (chaps. 17–18), or aspects of the millennium (chap. 20), or final outcomes (20:14; chaps. 21–22)—every significant item in the texture of the book is accompanied by at least one contextual clue showing it to be figurative.

Preterist Idealism

Our next task is to determine to what period of time the symbols point for their fulfillment. Do the clues require a preterist, an historicist, a futurist, or an idealist approach?

John sees the great end of the world quickly taking shape. He writes out of "tribulation" (1:9), and some in his audience are about to enter into "great tribulation" (2:10, 22; cf. 7:14). Christ threatens to come to the Asian churches as a "thief" (3:3) and to "war" against the disobedient with the "sword" of his mouth (2:16; cf. 19:15, 21). The hour of trial is enveloping the whole world; Christ will soon be here (3:10–11). Even now he is standing at the door and knocking (3:20; cf. Jas 5:9). The upshot will be the consummation of history (6:12–17; 7:15–17; 11:15–19; 14:14–20; 16:17–21; etc.). This consistent emphasis on last things may support a futuristic reading.

Yet with equal clarity John identifies the main actors in the drama as his contemporaries. The beast denotes provincial representatives of the emperor in Asia (13:1, 5–6; 17:9–10). The false prophet symbolizes priests of the ruler cult who require acts of obeisance to manufactured statues of the emperor as the condition for trading in marketplaces (13:12–17). The harlot is Roman society (17:4, 18; 18:11–17).

We can do justice to this union of present circumstance and apocalyptic scenario only by recognizing that John's method sets his addressees and their immediate crisis in the framework of a general eschatology. Facts of life in Roman Asia toward the close of the first century are the referents of the symbols; the symbols that do the referring carry the full significance of the final, cosmic showdown envisaged by the apocalyptic tradition. This clarifies the sense in which the prophecy "must soon take place" and "the time is near" (1:1, 3). At the time of writing readers are contending with forces that will bring about the end of the world. From this perspective, the much debated instruction, "Write what you see, what is and what is to take place hereafter" (1:19), does not refer to different parts of the book.[28] Rather the book as a whole, and each symbol in particular, sheds light on the present ("what is") by fusing it with the denouement of history ("what is to take place hereafter").[29]

To us, who have outlived John's prophecy by a margin of nearly two millennia and are still waiting for the end to come, this way of describing the moment seems overloaded and bombastic. In the cold light of history, the real actors did not match up to the grandiose personas bestowed upon them. In the opinion of a sizable swath of biblical critics, John was simply mistaken. These critics set aside the apocalyptic aspect of the work as so much disproven phantasmagoria, even if the prophecy is still worth studying for its expressions of great moral and spiritual truths.[30]

---

28. One popular exposition of the verse sees chapters 2–3 as exclusively concerned with "what is" and chapters 4–22 with "what is to take place hereafter." So, for example, Walvoord, *Revelation*, 47–49.

29. Beale, *Revelation*, 152–70.

30. For example, Charles, *Revelation*, 2.86; Beckwith, *Apocalypse*, 291–310.

This judgment, however, is facile, and has all but discredited preterism in the eyes of the many readers who hold the Revelation to be a true word from God. We shall be less hasty to see the Revelation as a body of failed predictions, to the extent that we recognize a foreshortened futurist perspective as typical of the biblical prophets.

Principle: Proximity of the Ultimate

All the prophets spoke of their own day in ultimate terms.[31] For example, each successor to the throne of Judah stepped at his coronation into a messianic penumbra (1 Chron 28:5; 29:20, 23; 2 Chron 9:8; Psa 2:7–9; 45:2–7; 72; 110), a hope that was deferred as each died in turn. For Isaiah, the twilight of the Assyrian empire, then of the Babylonian, would coincide with the collapse of the physical universe (Isa 13:10; 34:4); and the birth of an heir to the throne of King Ahaz (Isa 7:14–16; cf. 8:8) heralded the messianic kingdom (Isa 9:1–7). Joel's prophetic eye blended a current locust infestation (Joel 1–2) with an invasion of Palestine by all nations (Joel 2:4–11 [?]; 3:1–16). Ezekiel expected his eschatological temple (Ezek 40–44) to be the rallying point of the returning exiles (Ezek 43:10–11), but it remained an unrealized dream. Daniel perceived no interval between the ravages of Antiochus Epiphanes IV (Dan 11:21–39) and the "time of the end" (Dan 11:40ff.). Jesus capped his prediction of when the temple would be destroyed (Mark 13:1–23), which he said would be within a generation (v. 30), with a paragraph about the Parousia (Mark 13:24–27). One scene in the Revelation moves from the birth and ascension of Christ (Rev 12:1–5) directly into the tribulation period, without a gap (12:6–17).

Either the prophets were all deluded and their writings slipped into the canon of scripture by repeated errors of judg-

31. Beasley-Murray, *Revelation*, 47.

ment on the part of its guardians, or the advancing present stands in a profound relationship to the end of all things. If the biblical prophets seem to have exaggerated the magnitude of situations seen in retrospect to have been limited in time and place, that is because their faith discerned, in precisely their own circumstances, the same principles that await superlative actualization at the close of history.[32]

Technique: Reverse Typology

Biblical typology assumes the constancy of the divine character, the unity of human nature, and the continuity of God's dealings with people in all ages. Therefore the present may be depicted in terms of past events. There are numerous instances of typology in the book of Revelation. For example, Nicolaitan doctrine at contemporary Pergamum is called "the teaching of Balaam" (2:14), because the historic Balaam led Israel into the practice of idolatry (Num 25:1–3 in the light of 31:16). A false prophetess of Thyatira is styled "Jezebel" for a similar reason (Rev 2:20; 1 Kings 16:31; 21:25–26). And, as we saw above, the deliverance of John's churches can be presented under motifs from Israel's exodus saga.

Typology can also operate in reverse, in prophetic literature that stands in a tradition of shared apocalyptic images for the coming world-crisis. The present may be seen in the light of the future.

Assuming some Christians of Smyrna suffered imprisonment and a few became martyrs, like Antipas at Pergamum

32. Caird considers this to be a metaphorical use of end-of-the-world language to refer to what the authors knew was not the end of the world. See Caird, *Language and Imagery of the Bible*, 243–71, esp. 256. Whether John or former prophets in fact knew they were not referring to the end of the world is questionable. But had they known, would they have written differently?

(Rev 2:10, 13), admittedly they did not participate in the final tribulation that awaits the church. But their ordeal in the 90s and that of the end-time martyrs are of a piece, in significance if not in scale, and for their endurance they will receive the same crown. It was their "great tribulation" (2:10, 22; cf. 7:14).

If "Jezebel" contracted an illness (2:22), in one sense she did not encounter Christ at his Parousia and succumb to the sword of his mouth (2:16; cf. 19:15, 21). But Christ was no less truly her adversary and judge (cf. 1 Cor 11:30–31). It was her Armageddon. So completely did the religious sect surrounding the false prophetess of Thyatira pass off the scene that we are unable to reconstruct its tenets in any detail. Christ's word through his prophet prevailed (2:23).

How extensive is John's application of reverse typology will concern us in chapter six on the eschatology of the Apocalypse. The struggle of the Asian churches for Christian integrity in their Roman-Anatolian environment, and the last, titanic conflict between light and darkness that will mark the close of the age, coalesce in John's literary presentation, because the same nexus of theological principles is at stake. "Children, it is the last hour; and as you have heard that antichrist is coming, so now many antichrists have come" (1 John 2:18). The life of an individual or of a local community is a sort of microcosm of world history. In a very real sense, every generation faces the end. Today's pressures and decisions have eschatological import. Between a critically responsible preterist approach to the Revelation and the book's undeniably futuristic elements, idealism forms the bridge.[33]

John, by depicting his own time using ideas drawn from the apocalyptic stockpile, created a body of hyperboles, the full meaning of which has yet to be exhausted. His prophecy did not

33. Beasley-Murray, *Revelation*, 46–48; Osiek, "Apocalyptic Eschatology"; Noç, "Exegetical Basis for Preterist Idealism."

fall flat when the great catastrophe of the world did not come. For he did not set out to predict the date. He wanted to open his readers' eyes to the fateful nature of the here and now, as God sees it.

5

Main Theological Concepts

At a time when Christians in provincial Asia were being enticed and pressured to regard Roman culture as the locus of power, glory, wealth, and happiness, the Revelation shows that true glory exists in heaven where the invisible God exercises total control over affairs on earth through his unseen messianic king. The Apocalypse emphasizes aspects of the Christian view of reality that contradict Roman propaganda, and that call forth moral excellence in the midst of a degenerate society.[1]

GOD ALMIGHTY, CREATOR AND CONSUMMATOR[2]

Already in the prescript the main theological themes come to the fore.[3] Twice in that context, God is described as "he who is and who was and who is to come" (1:4, 8), a title that reverberates in the body of the Revelation (cf. 4:8; 11:17; 16:5). At the burning bush God had told Moses his name, "I AM WHO I AM" (Exod 3:14), claiming independent self-existence, sovereign self-determination, and immutability of character and purpose. To

---

1. Excellent overviews of the theology of the book of Revelation: Bauckham, *Theology of Revelation*; Osborne, *Revelation*, 31–49.

2. Bauckham, *Theology of Revelation*, 23–53; Rotz and Du Rand, "One Who Sits," 91–111.

3. De Smidt, "Meta-Theology."

the atemporal "who is" (reflecting "I AM"), the Apocalypse adds temporal phrases extending from eternity past ("who was") to eternity future ("who is to come"; cf. "King of the ages," 15:3).[4]

A second title underscores the first: "I am the Alpha and the Omega" (1:8). *Alpha* (A) and *omega* (Ω) are the first and last letters of the Greek alphabet. A similar statement is found at the latter end of the Apocalypse, followed by the parallel declaration that God is "the beginning and the end" (21:6). This *inclusio* undergirds all the promises in the book: promises of an end to wickedness, of God's presence, and of a new order of things in which sin, grief, death, mourning and pain shall have been done away (cf. 21:3–8).

Nine times God is entitled "the almighty (ὁ παντοκράτωρ [*ho pantokratōr*])" (1:8; 4:8; 11:17; 15:3; 16:7, 14; 19:6, 15; 21:22). This noun emphasizes God's ability to bring about anything he pleases, whether as creator (4:8–11), judge (11:18; 15:3–4; 16:5–7; 19:1–4), or ruler of the age to come (11:15–19; 19:6; 21:22). It states his omnipotence, and implies his omnipresence and omniscience.

John's vision of the throne-room of heaven (chaps. 4–5) occupies a sort of structural and theological apex of the Apocalypse.

	God and the Lamb in heaven (chaps. 4–5)	
Seven oracles (chaps. 2–3)		Scroll (chaps. 5–8; implied 5–22)
Christ in glory (1:9–20)		Little scroll (10–11; 12–15; 19–20)
Prescript (1:1–11)		Postscript (22:6–21)

The throne-room scene encapsulates the world view of the revelation.[5] By design, the qualifiers "almighty" and "who was and is and is to come" recur precisely here (4:8). Two more divine titles are introduced. "One seated on the throne" (4:2, 3, 9, 10;

4. McDonough, *YHWH at Patmos*.

5. Schimanowski, *Himmlische Liturgie*.

5:1, 7, 13) later becomes a favorite (6:16; 7:10, 15; 19:4; 20:11; 21:5; cf. "throne" 8:3; 12:5; 14:3; 16:17; 19:5; 22:1, 3). It is a pictorial representation of "the almighty." The one "who lives for ever and ever" (4:9, 10; 10:6; 15:7; cf. 7:2) has intrinsic life, in contrast to the lifeless idols of paganism (cf. 1 Thess 1:9).

Flashes of colored gems and a rainbow around the throne suggest the breathtaking radiance of the one who sits in state (4:3). His unapproachable majesty is illustrated by tiers of angels. Inmost are four living creatures (4:6–9),[6] corresponding to Old Testament seraphim (Isa 6:2–3) or cherubim (Ezek 1:5–21; 10), whose individual features represent all sectors of the sentient creation (Rev 4:7). Their chief raison d'etre is to praise God. Around them are twenty-four figures who follow the lead of the four in worship (4:4, 10; 5:8). That these too are angels is indicated by their mediate position in the retinue, by their sacerdotal role in the liturgy (5:8; cf. 8:3–4), and by their function as messengers of revelation to the human author (5:5; 7:13). Their number symbolizes a special affinity with the people of God in both testaments. That they are "elders" indicates them to be a council in charge of superintending the saints.[7] Beyond the senate of twenty-four are myriads of myriads and thousands of thousands of angels (5:11–12). A movement to acclaim God spreads outward in a great wave, starting from the seraphim nearest the throne, and taken up by cascading echelons of supernal beings one after another, until the choir encompasses everything in heaven and earth (5:8–14).

---

6. As constituents of the throne? The four living creatures may be conceived of on the analogy of engraved or sculpted components of ancient thrones. Hannah, "Cherubim and Throne," 530–41.

7. Their human features no more indicate them to be glorified human beings, than the features of the four living creatures indicate them to be heavenly animals. For a discussion of several other options concerning the identity of the 24 elders, see Aune, *Revelation*, 1.287–92.

Their praise of God has two foci. One hymn looks back to the divine work of creation (4:11). The other, inspired by the scroll and its contents about to be revealed (chap. 5), moves from redemption accomplished (5:9–10, 12) to the final destiny of all things (5:13–14).

This presentation of God as the one who established the world and determines its course is exactly what the churches of Asia needed to hear. It rivets attention away from the Roman imperium onto the actual monarch of the universe, shows that any human dominion is subordinate to and limited by an infinite authority in heaven, and exposes for a blasphemous farce the paying of obsequies to statues of the emperor.[8]

JESUS THE MESSIANIC KING[9]

Also broached in the prescript are some of the outstanding christological emphases of the Apocalypse. Jesus Christ was "the faithful witness" (1:5; cf. 3:14), the forerunner of Christians who were called upon in Roman courts of law to maintain the truth about who is in charge of the world (cf. John 18:36–37; 19:11; Rev 1:9; 2:13; 6:9; 11:3, 7; 12:11, 17; 17:6; 19:10; 20:4).

He is "the first-born of the dead" (1:5). Implicit in this phrase is the fact that Jesus was once dead (1:18; 2:8; 5:6, 9, 12; 13:8) by crucifixion (11:8), having shed his blood to redeem believers (5:9; 7:14; 12:11).[10] But he broke the sway of death and is now the living one (1:18; 2:8) who holds the keys of death and Hades (1:18).

---

8. Barnett, "Polemical Parallelism," 112–16; Morton, "Glory to God and Lamb"; Tóth, *Himmlische Kult*.

9. Bauckham, *Theology*, 54–65; Lioy, *Revelation in Christological Focus*.

10. Hanna, *Passione di Cristo*.

And he is "the ruler of kings on earth" (1:5). Following his birth, he was caught up to God and to his throne (12:5), whence he will come with the clouds to judge the tribes of the earth (1:7; cf. 14:14). Over against the caesars whose power was shored up ideologically by preposterous claims to be descendants of gods or to enjoy apotheosis at death, Jesus is revealed as the sole human being authorized to act as God's plenipotentiary. This emphasis on Jesus as God's mediatorial king is the most characteristic christological note of the book.

In the pivotal chapters 4–5, the Lamb is presented as the only one in heaven or on earth who is worthy, by virtue of his redemptive death (5:6, 9, 12), to unseal the scroll (5:1–7) that contains the divine plan for the close of the age. This is a narrative portrayal of the Johannine tenet that the Son of God is the unique executor of God's will, with special reference to the eschatological functions of eliminating opposition to the reign of God, resurrecting the dead and judging them (cf. John 5:17–29).

Accordingly, Jesus is the "Christ" who shares in God's supreme authority (11:15; 12:10; 20:6), "the King of kings and Lord of lords" (17:14; 19:16) who will fulfill Psalm 2:9 by smashing the nations with a rod of iron (2:27; 19:15, 20–21), the messianic regent of Jewish expectation out of whose mouth issues a sharp, two-edged sword with which to establish justice (1:16; 2:16; 19:15, 21; cf. Isa 11:4), the "root" and key holder of David (3:7; 5:5; 22:16; cf. Isa 11:1), the one like a son of man appointed to receive a kingdom with no boundary terrestrial or temporal (1:7, 13; 11:15; 14:14; cf. Dan 7:9–14).

This messianic kingdom is already realized in certain respects, albeit an invisible kingdom whose willing subjects still face tribulation and have to be long-suffering in this world (1:9). Jesus's instatement on the Father's throne is an accomplished event (3:21; 5:6; 7:9–10, 17; 12:5). His nullification of the diabolic accuser once and for all by means of his blood inaugurated the salvation and the power and the kingdom of God, and the authority of God's Christ (12:10). He is the Lamb with seven horns, and even now he sends out the seven spirits of God into all the earth (5:6). In other respects, however, the kingdom will only be fully realized at the end of the present age, when the raging of the nations is ended, the destroyers of the earth are destroyed, the dead are judged and the servants of God have received their rewards (11:15–18; 20:10–21:8).

Does Jesus Christ belong to the ambit of deity? With God he shares the titles "Alpha and Omega" and "the beginning and the end" (22:13; cf. 1:8; 21:6), to which is joined "the first and the last" (1:17; 2:8; 22:13). Though he never receives the appellation of "almighty," there is in the Revelation, in keeping with exclusive monotheism, a single divine throne, and Jesus shares it with his Father. The natural force of the Greek in 5:1 is, "I saw in the midst of the throne . . . a Lamb"; that this is the sense is confirmed by similar expressions elsewhere (cf. 3:21; 7:17; 22:1, 3).[11] An Old Testament portrait of the divine judge with hair like white wool (Dan 7:9) supplies imagery for Jesus (Rev 1:14). The Lamb has seven eyes that are the seven spirits of God sent out into the earth (3:1; 5:6). He is associated with God as an object of adoration (5:13; 7:9–10), and as the agent of eschatological wrath (6:16–17; 14:14–16). At 2:18 he is "the Son of God." He has a name that is a wonder known only to himself (19:12), and his title "the Word of God" (19:13) parallels John 1:1, "In the beginning was the Word, and the Word was with God, and the Word was God."[12]

---

11. Hannah, "Cherubim and Throne"; "Throne of His Glory," 68–71.

12. Bauckham, "Worship of Jesus," in *Climax*, 118–49; Hengel, "Throngemeinschaft"; Söding, "Gott und Lamm."

How, then, does he have angelic attributes?[13] The opening christophany (1:13–16) picks up several descriptive phrases from Daniel's record of the appearance of Gabriel (Dan 10:5–6). Also an angel at 10:1–3 has been thought by some commentators so impressive that he must be Christ himself. Yet John is in no doubt as to the qualitative distinction between divinity and angels, between that incomparable being to whom worship is due and those creatures who, as brethren of the saints, stand with them in worshipping God alone (19:10; 22:8–9). As a monotheist he is not likely to have confused angels with God or Christ.[14] Contrary to the christological interpretation of 10:1–3, the figure there is indeed an "angel," as the author states plainly (10:1), graced with visionary features of the God whose message he bears (cf. Ezek 1:4, 27–28), even as apparitions of the angel of the LORD in the Old Testament could speak in the first person in God's name (Exod 3:2, 6; Josh 5:14 with 6:2). This suggests a solution to the earlier passage as well. The entire Revelation was made known to John through the agency of an angel (1:1; 22:8). In 1:10–16, it may be this angel appearing to John under a form emblematic of Christ to convey words from Christ. On John's mistaking the agent for the very person of Christ and prostrating himself, the angel sets the record straight (19:10; 22:8–9).

THE SPIRIT OF PROPHECY[15]

Nowhere in the Apocalypse does the phrase "Holy Spirit" crop up. Instead we find simply "the Spirit" (Rev 1:10; 2:7, 11, 17, 29; 3:6, 13, 22; 4:2; 14:13; 17:3; 21:10; 22:17). With respect to this usage the Revelation is like the Fourth Gospel and the

13. Carrell, *Jesus and the Angels*.
14. Stuckenbruck, *Angel Veneration*; Hoffmann, *Destroyer and Lamb*.
15. Bauckham, *Theology*, 109–25; Aune, *Revelation*, 1.36.

Johannine epistles, which together have "Holy Spirit" very few times (John 1:33; 14:26; 20:22).

A peculiarity of the Revelation is several references to "seven" spirits (1:4; 3:1; 4:5; 5:6). The divine Spirit is meant.[16] In the prescript, the seven spirits are sandwiched between "him who is, etc." and Jesus Christ, in what must be a Trinitarian greeting (1:4–5). Addition of the qualifying phrase "of God," to yield "seven spirits of God" (3:1; 4:5; 5:6), creates a title that corresponds to the more familiar biblical "Spirit of God" (e.g., 1 John 4:2). Their abode is before the throne in heaven (1:4; 4:5), where they appear as burning torches (4:5), a visionary equivalent to the adjective "Holy." They are the eyes, or conscious understanding, of the Lamb, mediating his presence on earth (5:6). The seven spirits, then, are a graphic representation (cf. Zech 4:2, 6, 10) of the seven potencies of the Holy Spirit listed in a key verse of the Old Testament (LXX Isa 11:2), the number seven denoting fullness.[17]

The Spirit is associated with God ("before his throne," ". . . of God"), and also with the Son of God (3:1; 5:6), even as in the Fourth Gospel the Father sends the Spirit in the Son's name (John 14:25) while the Son sends him from the Father (John 15:26).

But the stress of the Apocalypse falls on the Spirit's role in giving prophecy to and through the church.[18] In four instances John is said to be "in the Spirit" when he receives revelations (1:10; 4:2; 17:3; 21:10). Nine other times, verbal oracles are ascribed to the Spirit (2:7, 11, 17, 29; 3:6, 13, 22; 14:13; 22:17).

16. De Smidt, "Acts of God and Spirit Rev 1:4."

17. For an assertion that the seven spirits are not divine but are to be identified with the seven angels of 8:2, see Aune, *Revelation*, 1.33–35. Aune dismisses as "artificial and unconvincing" the biblical backgrounds usually adduced to support the Trinitarian understanding.

18. Bauckham, "Role of the Spirit," in *Climax*, 150–73; Waddell, *Spirit in Revelation*.

These passages are summed up in the statement, "The testimony of Jesus is the Spirit of prophecy" (19:10 [capital "s" mine]). As we saw in our first chapter, John regarded his writing as a prophecy (1:3, 9; 10:11; 22:7, 10, 16, 18, 19), aware that he stood in a prophetic tradition (10:7) and was one of a special body of prophets (22:6, 9) serving a church whose witness is a prophetic one in this world (2:13; 6:9; 11:3, 6, 7, 10, 18; 12:11; 16:6; 18:20, 24; 20:4), as Jesus Christ's was (1:5; 3:14). "The testimony of Jesus" (cf. 1:2, 9; 12:17; 20:4) is, then, both the witness Jesus bears to himself (subjective genitive), and the witness to him borne by John and other followers of Jesus (objective genitive), empowered by the same Spirit who moved the prophets. John thinks of the Spirit in the concrete, as indwelling the church and enabling her to prophesy boldly in the midst of hostility (11:3–7, 10).[19]

THE CHURCH—PRESERVED YET BUFFETED[20]

Consideration of the Spirit leads directly into John's teaching about the church. A foundation for ecclesiology is laid down in the prescript. Jesus has made believers "a kingdom, priests to his God and Father" (1:6; cf. 3:9; 5:10). These words hark back to the charter of Israel at Mount Sinai, where God promised to make his chosen nation "a kingdom of priests" (Exod 19:6). Thus the very definition of Israel as the special people chosen by God to bring his ruling and sanctifying grace to all nations, now belongs to the people associated with Israel's messiah. John is at one with previous New Testament authors in seeing organic continuity between the faithful of the old and the new covenants (Acts 15:14–19;

---

19. Barnett, "Polemical Parallelism," 119.
20. Tavo, "Ecclesial Notions."

Rom 2:29; 11:17–24; Gal 6:16; Eph 2:11—3:6; Phil 3:3; Col 2:11; Heb 13:10, 13–15; 1 Pet 2:9–10).[21]

Predicates of Israel are again transferred to the church in the passage about the sealing of the 144,000 (7:4–8). This paragraph metaphorically applies to the church Israel's archaic tribal divisions dating from the time of the Egyptian plagues and exodus, to make the point that the church is similarly elect and cherished by God, and will enjoy his protection from the plagues that are coming (7:3; 9:4; cf. Exod 9:7, 26; 12:13). Although a superficial reading may give the impression that the paragraph is about Jews only, painstaking comparison of the details with lists of the twelve tribes found in the Old Testament (Gen 29:31—30:24; 35:22–26; 46:8–27; 49:2–27; Exod 1:2–5; Num 1:5–15, 20–43; 2:1–31; Josh 13–19, etc.) discloses subtle adjustments in John's New Testament perspective.[22] On the numerology, see above, pp. 56–57. The census in 7:5–8 is a

---

21. Wojciechowski, "Church as Israel"; Mayo, *Who Call Themselves Jews*.

22. Here Judah precedes the other tribes (7:5), even though he was the fourth born to Jacob, because Christ has come from his stock (cf. Rev 5:5). Simeon and Levi, Jacob's second and third sons, fall much further down in John's list (7:7) because the issue of primogeniture is now moot. Dan and Ephraim are omitted because of their historic association with idolatrous shrines at Dan and Bethel (1 Kings 12:29). John wants to discourage the churches from participating in Greco-Roman idolatry (2:14, 20; 9:20; 21:8; 22:15). To make up for these two omissions, the priestly tribe of Levi, formerly deleted from the old inheritance lists (Num 1:47–54; Deut 10:8–9; Josh 14:3–5), is restored, since the issue of land inheritance is no longer a live one; and Joseph takes the place of his son Ephraim, creating the curiosity that Joseph and his other son, Manasseh, both find places in John's list (7:6, 8), for which there is no precedent in any Old Testament passage.

symbolic vehicle for theological truths that John wants to drive home to the Christian churches of his day.[23]

Side by side with the 144,000 is another vision, of a multicultural throng praising God and the Lamb in heaven (7:9–17). This is a picture, not of a different subject, but of the same body of people to make a different point about them.[24] If the first part of chapter 7 brings out the distinctiveness of God's elect in the midst of a society ripe for punishment (cf. 6:15–17), the latter part highlights the ethnic diversity and inclusiveness of the group who receive salvation.

A twin emphasis on having peace in Christ yet tribulation in the world (cf. John 16:33) is another theme of John's ecclesiology. Shielded from God's plagues (7:1–8), the church nevertheless endures tribulation from its pagan neighbors (6:9–11; 7:14). The church is the temple of God (11:1–2; see 1:20; 3:12; 7:15; 21:3, 22; and cf. 1 Cor 3:16; 1 Pet 2:5). Its holy interior—its God-ward relation—is preserved during the three-and-a-half years (11:1), while its outer court—its exposure to the world—is trampled by heathen (11:2).[25] So also the celestial woman who represents the idea or essence of the people of God corporate is herself kept from the dragon (12:4–6, 13–16), but her children draw his fury (12:17) through the instrumentality of the beast (13:7, 10).

In 14:1–5 those with the Lamb stand in direct antithesis to the mass of earth dwellers who submit to the beast (cf. 13:3–4, 8, 12), and so the motif of the chosen 144,000 comes into play again. Here the 144,000 on Mount Zion are explicitly identified as the church: they are those who bear the name of the Lamb and

---

23. Smith, "Portrayal of Church as New Israel"; Bauckham, "List of Tribes."

24. Dalrymple, "These Are the Ones."

25. Tavo, "Outer and Inner Court Rev 11:1–2."

of his Father (14:1; cf. Matt 28:19), who have been redeemed from the earth (Rev 14:3; cf. 5:9), who follow the Lamb without question (cf. Mark 8:34), and are first fruits to God (14:4; cf. Rom 8:23; Jas 1:18). Virginity (14:4) is a symbol of abstention from the godlessness of Roman society (14:8; 17:5; 18:3 etc.) so that they are fit to become the bride of the Lamb (19:7–8; 21:9).[26] Their truth-telling (14:5) contrasts with the fawning of the many who flatter the beast (13:4, 12).

Ecclesiological motifs of the whole book flow together in the unveiling of Lady Jerusalem at its close (21:9—22:9). This vision consists of two carefully worked-out, seven-part chiastic structures that shed light on each other, one underscoring the election of the community of the redeemed to be holy (21:11–22), the other the diffusion of its royal glory to the nations (21:23—22:5).

---

26. In the context of 14:4 the faithful are represented as males who have abstained from relations with "women," probably a reference to Lady Babylon who will be introduced into the narrative in v. 8. Harlotry is a common Old Testament metaphor for idolatry, and the symbolism of virginity may also resonate with the depiction of God's people as a maiden qualified by virtue of her purity for marriage to the Lamb (19:7–8; 21:2, 9). Zimmermann, "Virginitäts-Metapher Apk 14:4–5."

Election of the city to be holy (21:11–22)
   Presence of God (v. 11)
     Gates (vv. 12–13)—names of the patriarchs of Israel
       Wall-foundations (v. 14)—names of the twelve apostles
         City dimensions (vv. 15–18)—cubical and squared values
           denoting inner sanctum (1 Kings 6:20; 2 Chron 3:8)
       Wall-foundations (vv. 19–20)—cf. high-priestly breastplate
         (Exod 28:17–21)
     Gates (v. 21)—pearls (cf. Matt 13:45–46)
   Presence of God (v. 22)
Diffusion of royal glory of the city (21:23—22:5)
   God its light (21:23)
     Nations serve the King (vv. 24–26)
       Exclusion of abominations from the city (v. 27)
         River and tree of life for healing of the nations (22:1–2)
       Exclusion of accursed things from the city (v. 3a)
     Servants attend the King (vv. 3b–4)
   God its light (v. 5)

"City" (21:10), then, is itself a symbol of the community of the redeemed, and does not denote a physical place.[27]

In summary, the rich ecclesiology of the Apocalypse is woven out of a number of dual threads: the people of God are old/new, Israelite/multinational, royal/hieratic, special/inclusive, sustained/persecuted.

THE ADVERSARIES

Over against God, his Christ, and the prophetic Spirit in the Church, have arisen evil forces within God's creation that op-

---

27. Dumbrell, *End of the Beginning*, 35–164; Bauckham, *Theology of Revelation*, 126–43; Lee, *New Jerusalem*.

pose God's purposes in the combat of the ages: the devil, the emperor, the priests of the imperial cult, and dwellers on earth. Each is a travesty of its divine or godly counterpart.[28]

If God has a surpassing beauty (4:3), the devil appears as a hideous red dragon with seven snake-like heads and ten horns (12:3, 9). The seven heads and ten horns indicate an aspiration to universal dominion, in rivalry to God. Therefore the dragon, in dread of God's plan, tries to devour the messiah at birth, but fails and instead gets cast down out of heaven (12:4–12).

God rules through his Christ. So also the dragon has an earthly organ through whom he carries out his malevolent designs. He calls forth a beast from the depths of the sea (12:17—13:1), whose proper abode is the abyss (11:7; 17:8). Like the dragon, it has ten horns and seven heads, to signify their intimate collusion in seeking totalitarian empire (13:1, 4; 17:3, 7), and to mimic the Lamb with seven horns (5:6). Its name and its mouth are blasphemous (13:1, 5–6; 17:3), in that it sets itself forth as divine and basks in receiving worship (13:4, 14–15; cf. Dan 11:36–37; 2 Thess 2:4). The beast is the Roman emperor (17:9–10) as the contemporary avatar of all empires that have oppressed the people of God (13:2; cf. Dan 7:1–8). Even as the Lamb was slain yet rose again (5:6; 1:18), so also the beast suffers a mortal wound yet proves resilient, striking awe in the whole earth (13:3).[29] It makes war on the saints and conquers them (13:7), a figure for its opposition to the church (13:10; 14:12–13).[30]

28. Poythress, "Counterfeiting."

29. Debate has not yet settled over whether the myth of Nero's return from death to lead an invasion of the empire had gelled sufficiently in the 90s to serve as a source of John's language. See Aune, *Revelation*, 2.737–40. Favoring some degree of influence from a myth still in formation is Klauck, "Do They Never Come Back?"

30. Bauckham, "Apocalypse as a Christian War Scroll," in *Climax*, 210–37.

In contrast to the Spirit-inspired, prophetic Church that tells the truth about God and does not lie (14:5; 21:27; 22:15), the state religion presents the exterior of a lamb but speaks like a dragon (13:11), and so gains the title of "false prophet" (16:13; 19:20; 20:10). Its officers direct people to perform acts of worship to the emperor (13:12), using all means of deception to produce counterfeit signs and wonders associated with imperial effigies (13:13–15; cf. Matt 24:23–24; 2 Thess 2:9–12).

These efforts are successful in persuading "every tribe and people and tongue and nation" and "all who dwell on earth" to clamor after the beast (13:7–8, 14), in particular "the kings of the earth" who represent the various peoples (16:13–14; 17:12; 19:18–19). Not only do they cooperate with Rome's political will, they buy into Rome's prosperity. The kings of the earth greedily "commit fornication" with Babylon the mother of harlots (14:8; 17:2, 18; 18:3, 9). Followers of the beast among the general populace gladly receive the mark 666 on their right hands or their foreheads so that they can buy and sell freely (13:16–18). Thus "these worshipers of the beast and its image" (14:11) make up a community in antithesis to the 144,000 chosen whose foreheads are marked with the name of God and of the Lamb, who are virgins.[31]

Just as the Fourth Gospel confronts the reader with polarities between life and death, light and darkness, truth and falsehood, with no shades of gradation, so the Revelation urges an ineluctable choice between stark alternatives.[32] Either the hearer will belong to the race of Jerusalem, imbued with the prophetic Spirit sent into the world by Christ from God; or will be a mem-

---

31. Rossing, *Choice Between Two Cities*; Campbell, "Antithetical Women-Cities."

32. Kramer, "Contrast as Key to Understanding."

ber of the race of Babylon, listening to the false prophet deputed by the beast in Rome who is the ape of the dragon.

Race of Jerusalem	Race of Babylon
Spirit(s) of God	False prophet
Christ-Lamb	Beast
God Almighty	(Dragon's aspiration)

Another characteristic of both the Apocalypse and the other Johannine literature is a tendency to mull over a select body of critically important theological ideas, penetrating to the nub of those ideas.

SALVATION

Finally, what must one do to be found on the winning side in the combat, to "conquer" (2:7, 11, 17, 26; 3:5, 12, 21; 12:11; 15:2; 21:7) and insure one's place in the new Jerusalem?

Victory for the saints is grounded in the fact that the Lamb has already conquered by his blood (5:5, 9; 12:11), and is destined to conquer in the visible, public realm by the breath of his mouth (17:14; cf. 19:15, 21). The blood of the Lamb has freed us from our sins (1:5) and ransomed people for God from every nation (5:9; cf. "redeemed," 14:4), washing their filthy robes white (7:14).

Back of the Lamb's inaugurated victory is the eternal divine plan to save those whose names were written in the book of life before the foundation of the world (17:8) by the slaying of the Lamb whose sacrifice was appointed to that end (13:8). Thus although the keynote of the prophecy will be an exhortation to the churches to persevere, ultimately their final salvation is grounded in the pre-cosmic purpose of God.

On that basis, John exhorts his readers to persevere in "following" the Lamb wherever he goes (14:4). "Endurance" is paramount (1:9), both in commendations of churches (2:2–3, 19; 3:10), and in exhortations (13:10; 14:12), as is "holding on" (2:25; 3:11).[33] A reward is in store for the one who keeps Christ's works "until the end" (2:26–28).

Christ is constantly evaluating the "works" of those who profess his name to see whether they measure up, and those whose works fall short come in for stern admonishment before it is too late for them to repent (2:5, 6, 19, 22, 23, 26; 3:1, 2, 8, 15). Christians are characterized as those who keep the commandments of God (12:17; 14:12). Refusal to repent of abominable works is a sure sign of those headed for destruction (2:5, 16, 21–22; 3:3; 9:20–21; 16:9, 11; 18:6). For "works" will be the criterion at the final judgment, because works will be the corroborating evidence in support of names written in the Lamb's book of life (20:12–13; 22:12). As for those who die in the Lord, their works follow with them (14:13). The outcome of the Last Assize will be a division of the human race into those who proceed into the eternal city, and those who proceed into the lake of fire, according to what each has done (20:13).

Special accents fall on ethical issues that John and the churches of Asia were facing in the 90s. They must renew the warmth of their love (2:4), clean up their deeds and make them good (3:4, 18), abstain from the idolatry and fornication that were prevalent in their environment (2:6, 14–16, 20–23; 9:20–21; 21:8; 22:15), and resist the beast and its mark (14:9–11; 15:2). For some, following the Lamb wherever he goes in a society poisoned by the influence of the beast will mean imprisonment (2:10) or even martyrdom (2:10, 13; 6:9–11; 11:7–10; 13:7, 10; 16:6; 17:6; 18:24; 19:2; 20:4).

33. Campbell, "Apocalypse Johannique et Persévérance Des Saints."

Remarkably, the verb "to believe" does not occur in the Revelation. The noun "faith" is there twice as a virtue (2:19; 13:10) and twice in the sense of a religious affiliation to Christ (2:13; 14:12), in contexts that have to do with loyalty and perseverance. More typical is the adjective "faithful," which ties in with the theme of endurance (2:10, 13; 17:14). The book of Revelation is not, for the most part, an evangelistic document (though note the invitation to "come" at 22:17). It was addressed to Christians who had already professed belief in Jesus, with a view to steeling them for the rigors of following the Lamb in a society that had scant sympathy for their cause. Nothing less was at stake than whether they would spend eternity in Jerusalem, or outside it (22:14–15).

Our salvation, then, is determined from beginning to end by the Almighty who is and was and is to come, it was provided for by the death of the Lamb, and it remains contingent upon our hearing what the Spirit says to the churches and persevering all the way. In realizing the Father's soteriological plan the objective agent is the Son who acts in history, and the subjective agent is the Spirit who elicits a response of "coming" and of ongoing works from the human heart. The three conspire. Without any one of the factors in the triune operation, there would be no salvation. Where the three cooperate, salvation is assured.

6

Eschatology

ESCHATOLOGY, THE study of the last things, might well have been included among the theological concepts covered in chapter five. But a greater percentage of the Apocalypse than of any other book of the New Testament consists of eschatological language. Also, people who want to systematize biblical teaching about the end often turn to the Apocalypse. For these reasons, the eschatology deserves a chapter of its own.

It needs to be pointed out right at the outset that to teach eschatology as such is not the purpose of the book of Revelation. As every chapter above has stressed, the Revelation was a call to the churches of western Asia Minor during the reign of Domitian to persevere in Christian speech and conduct in the teeth of pressures to conform to Roman values, and it depicts scenes of the final cataclysm to that end. It makes use of an accepted scheme of end-time events that John expected his readers to know and recognize, but it does not break ground in that area. Had the author wished to lay down a new and fuller doctrine of the last things, why should he scramble the scheme into so many confusing cycles?[1] To reiterate makes sense if he is hammering home an urgent summons to repent, be steadfast, and maintain integrity; but not if he meant to enable the churches see more clearly the shape of the future, as in a crystal ball.

1. See chapter three above, pp. 28–44.

Because of the complexity of the Revelation, vastly different systems of eschatology have based themselves on it and entered into debate with others. It is a mistake to start from the Revelation in the New Testament, or from Daniel in the Old, and work backwards into the respective testaments when putting together an account of the eschatology of scripture. Both books present formidable interpretive knots. If we take them as our starting-points, we run the danger of reading into them preconceived ideas.

One long-standing rule of thumb for interpreting scripture is to proceed from clear passages to obscure ones, not vice versa.[2] Another is to trace the development of revelation in history. John is conscious that the visions vouchsafed to him form the last statement in the cumulative record of biblical prophecy (Rev 10:7). To fit together the fragments of eschatology that we find scattered in his work, it is necessary to bring to our study of the Apocalypse a pre-understanding of what earlier contributors to the canon of scripture had to say on the subject. If we do that, many pieces of the puzzle fall into place.

PRE-UNDERSTANDING FROM THE OLD TESTAMENT[3]

When we note the gradual advances of biblical authors in conceptualizing the last things, several observations stand out. Again and again, saints look to God to deliver them from present troubles and make them secure in the kingdom of his justice. Usually they envisage God's final kingdom as more or less imminent, with no long interval between themselves and the

---

2. Augustine, *On Christian Doctrine* 2.9 (14) (*NPNF*¹ 2:539); 3.2 (2) (*NPNF*¹ 2:556–57).

3. A fuller survey of Old Testament eschatology can be found in Beckwith, *Apocalypse*, 3–82.

end. Therefore as one generation succeeds another, the eschatological horizon keeps receding. The content of expectation is continually revised to reflect ever more mature understandings of the ways of God.

According to the pre-diluvial saga in Genesis, the very basic hope given to Adam and Eve after their fall was that, although the serpent would wound the heel of Eve's offspring, the offspring would eventually wound the serpent's head (Gen 3:15). Eve at first may have seen this hope coming to fulfillment in the birth of Cain (Gen 4:1),[4] but had to shift it to Seth (Gen 4:25–26). Some generations later, Lamech saw, beyond the cursed ground and its toils, relief on its way through Noah (Gen 5:29). But Noah was not the final deliverer either. The blessing would come through his son Shem (Gen 9:26).

God's blessing took on sharper definition when he promised the land of Canaan to Abram and his descendants (Gen 12:1–3; 13:14–17), to become their inheritance after four hundred years of servitude in Egypt (Gen 15:13–20). Abraham could appeal to God's righteousness as "the Judge of all the earth" (Gen 18:25), and purchased a family burial ground among the Hittites in anticipation (Gen 23). His grandson Jacob in Egypt singled out a scepter-bearer from the tribe of Judah as the one whom the peoples would obey (Gen 49:10).

In the event, however, hope was deferred again. Although the song of Moses and Miriam after the exodus spoke of God's kingdom being established in the promised land (Exod 15:17–18), Balaam's oracle interposed a series of nations that would dispossess one another before a star should come forth out of Jacob (Num 24:17–24). It took a full generation of conquest before the land was in Israelite control according to the Abrahamic

4. If Kaiser's suggestion can stand that Eve's exclamation in Genesis 4:1 be translated, "I have gotten a man, *even* YHWH." *OT Theology*, 37, 79.

promise (Josh 21:43–45), and centuries more of checkered fortunes before David rose at last as regent on God's behalf in Jerusalem (2 Sam 7; Psa 18:43–50; 78:65–72).

Yet the monarchy of Judah failed to produce the expected utopia. When David died, hopes attached to Solomon (1 Chron 28:5; 29:20, 23; Psa 72), but to no avail, and the nation divided. Much later, when the southern kingdom was threatened by a Syro-Ephraimite coalition from the north, Isaiah saw messianic potential in the birth of a royal scion, probably Hezekiah (Isa 7:14–16; 8:1–8; 9:1–7; chap. 11). Deliverance came, but the messiah did not. In due course, Nebuchadnezzar invaded the land and carried off the royalty to Babylonia. Among the Jewish exiles, optimism gathered around Jehoiachin when he was promoted to the king's table (2 Kings 25:27–29); among those who returned, around Zerubbabel when Persia appointed him governor (Hag 2:20–23; Zech 3:8; 6:9–14). But the kingdom remained in the future.

Daniel in exile thought the time of Jerusalem's devastation was drawing to a close around 539 B.C. based on his computation of Jeremiah's seventy years (Dan 9:1–19; Jer 25:11–12; 29:10). But an angelic message reinterpreted that figure to a mystical seventy times seven (Dan 9:20–27). By other dreams it was revealed that four empires had yet to hold hegemony over God's people before the termination of the world (Dan 2), the last of which would produce an especially virulent persecutor (Dan 7; 9:20–27). In this most elaborate of Old Testament eschatologies, the kingdom of God, administered by one like a son of man, displaces all that went before it, as a fifth, everlasting empire (Dan 2:34–35, 44–45; 7:7:9–14, 27).

Out of these expectations we can distill a core eschatology of the Old Testament. After a period of affliction for Israel during which she is overwhelmed by enemies, God will intervene, regathering his displaced people and setting up his eternal kingdom, headed by a Davidic king, in the land of promise (Isa 65:17—66:24; Jer 23:5–6; 33:14–26; Ezek 43:7; Dan 7:14), from which blessings will stream outwards to all nations (Isa 2:1–4; Mic 4:1–8).[5] Certain events came to be associated with the divine intervention, especially a battle royal to defend the holy people against gentile aggressors on the soil of Palestine (Joel 3:1–16; Ezek 38–39; Zech 12:1–9; 14:1–5), a resurrection of the deceased faithful (Isa 26:19; Dan 12:2), and a general judgment (Psa 7:6–8; Jer 25:15–38; Dan 7:9–12). No single passage contains a synthesis of all elements, but several give a rough outline (Isa 24–27; Joel 3; Ezek 37–48; Dan 7:1–14 with 11:40—12:3; Zech 14).

PRE-UNDERSTANDING FROM THE NEW TESTAMENT[6]

Jesus proclaimed the arrival of the kingdom of God (Mark 1:15; Luke 11:20; Matt 12:28). His disciples, identifying him as the messiah (Mark 8:29), at first expected him to usher in the Israelite kingdom directly (Luke 19:11; 24:21; Acts 1:6; cf. John 6:15). They had to modify their expectation in the light of his Ascension to heaven, which inaugurated a first, invisible phase of the kingdom, to be completed at his second coming in power (Acts 1:11; 3:21). Later New Testament authors took over the conviction that the essence of the kingdom of God had already come (Rom 14:17; Col 1:13; Heb 12:28).[7]

---

5. The prophets of Judah consistently looked for a universal kingdom of God on earth that would be everlasting in duration (e.g., Isa 9:7; 65:17–25; Ezek 43:7; Dan 7:14; Mic 4:1–8). These Old Testament prophecies correspond to Revelation 21:9—22:5, not to the millennium of 20:1–6, as dispensationalism erroneously holds.

6. Beckwith, *Apocalypse*, 82–156.

7. Glasson, "Temporary Messianic Kingdom."

What remains to transpire is given in Jesus's eschatological discourse (Matt 24//Mark 13//Luke 21) and in some of his parables. According to the Olivet discourse, a siege of Jerusalem would conclude the tribulation, and Jesus's coming on the clouds with glory would follow on its heels. In retrospect, the Parousia not having taken place in A.D. 70, two fulfillments of Jesus's words, a preterite and an eschatological, have to be distinguished. In speaking of the "desolating sacrilege" (Matt 24:15//Mark 13:14), Jesus used an expression that could refer equally to the desecration of the temple by the Romans (Luke 21:20–24), and to some unspecified violation of the temple of the new covenant, the church (cf. 2 Thess 2:4). He taught the following scheme.

	Olivet discourse	Tares	Sheep/goats
Social distresses	Matt 24:4–14// Mark 13:5–13// Luke 21:8–19		
The tribulation	Matt 24:15–28// Mark 13:14–23// Luke 21:20–25		
Portents	Matt 24:29// Mark 13:24–25// Luke 21:25–26		
Parousia	Matt 24:30–31// Mark 13:26–27// Luke 21:27	Matt 13:41	Matt 25:31
Judgment	Matt 24:45–51// Luke 21:34–36	Matt 13:40–42	Matt 25:31–46
Eternal kingdom		Matt 13:43	Matt 25:46

Paul did not alter this simple series of events. His advice to single persons not to marry was founded on a sense that the tribulation might be about to start (1 Cor 7:26–31). Until late in his ministry he anticipated the Parousia within his lifetime (1 Thess 4:15; 1 Cor 15:51–52), a stance he reconsidered after brushes with death (2 Cor 1:8; 5:1; Phil 1:19–26; 2 Tim 4:6). He echoed Daniel in expecting a "lawless one" who will be active during the tribulation (2 Thess 2:3–12), and taught that the resurrection-transformation of believers will happen at the Parousia of Christ (1 Thess 4:13–18; 1 Cor 15:23; Phil 3:21), as will the final judgment with its eternal issues (2 Thess 1:6–10; Rom 2:5–16).

The author of the Fourth Gospel, like Paul, knew of a time of tribulation coming on the church (John 14:1; 15:18—16:4; 16:33), to be followed by Jesus's return to receive his beloved ones (John 14:2–3). There will be a general resurrection and judgment of the good and of the evil (John 5:28–29) on "the last day" (John 6:39, 40, 44, 54; 11:24; 12:48). The final state of the saints will be with Christ in his glory (John 17:24).

To the Old Testament eschatology, then, the New Testament adds only christological and ecclesiological accents. It redefines the suffering and to-be-vindicated people of God so as to exclude Jews who do not believe in Jesus, and include gentiles who do.[8] It clarifies that Jesus Christ will be the focal agent of the coming theophany, leading to a triumph over God's foes, the resurrection, the judgment, and the unveiling of the eternal kingdom. While the end has drawn near in Christ, the New Testament writers do not delimit the period within which we are to look for him.[9]

ESCHATOLOGY IN THE APOCALYPSE

If our analysis of the literary structure of the Apocalypse (chapter three above) was correct in concluding that chapters 6–22 of Revelation are cyclical, we can now posit a basic scheme of

8. Mayo, *Who Call Themselves Jews*.
9. Moore, *Parousia in NT*.

events that informs the several recapitulating series, a scheme organic with the eschatological teaching of the Old and the New Testaments.

	Seals	Trumpets	Combat1	Bowls	Babylon	Combat2	Jerusalem
Social disturbances	6:1–8						
Persecution of saints	6:9–11		12:6–14:5		17:3–13		
Portents	6:12–14	8:6–13		15:5–16:12			
Muster for Armageddon		9:1–19		16:13–16			
Parousia/ Armageddon	6:15–17	11:15–18	14:14–20		17:14	19:10–21; 20:7–10	
Cosmic destruction	8:1–5			16:17–21	17:15–19:5		
Resurrection		11:18 (implied)				20:4–6; 20:13	
Judgment		11:18				20:11–14	
Kingdom / new creation		11:15, 19			19:6–8	21:1–8	21:9–22:5

Like the prophets who preceded him, the Seer is, for the most part, aware of little temporal space between himself and the eschatological events he describes (according to the general principle of the proximity of the ultimate), and sees some of them as irrupting into the present (using reverse typology). A few of these items are of special interest and call for a closer look.

THE TRIBULATION

Twice the Apocalypse speaks of "*the* tribulation" (with article) as an item already known to readers (1:9; 7:14; cf. Mark 13:14–23; 2 Thess 2:3–12). Both references involve believers suffering for their faith. John and his readers are experiencing "tribulation," qualified by "kingdom" and "endurance" (1:9). Also a throng of worshipers whom the author sees assembled before God's heavenly throne from all over the world are said to have come out of "the great tribulation" (7:14).

What kinds of suffering this tribulation entails for the church include: being pursued (12:13), not being allowed to buy or sell in market places without demonstrating loyalty to the beast (13:16), being slandered to civic authorities by Jewish informers (2:9; 3:9), arrests (13:10), imprisonments (2:10), exile for the word of God—presumably for preaching it (1:9)—and martyrdoms (2:13; 6:9–11; 13:15; 16:6; 17:6; 18:24; 19:2; 20:4).

Perpetrating these outrages are the beasts, political and religious, inspired by the dragon (chap. 13); and Roman society, symbolized by the harlot (17:6; 18:24). Nowhere in the Revelation does the noun "antichrist" occur, but Christian interpreters quickly borrowed the term from the Johannine epistles (1 John 2:18, 22; 4:3; 2 John 7) and attached it to these characters.[10] Their hostility to Christianity is represented symbolically as a war conducted against the saints (Rev 11:7; 12:17; 13:7). This is a new application of phraseology from Daniel where it had to do with actual military campaigns of the Seleucid kingdom against Judaea (Dan 7:21; 8:10, 12, 24–25; 9:26; 11:25).

Three-and-a-half years is the length of the conflict, variously given as "forty-two months" (Rev 11:2; 13:5), 1260 days (11:3; 12:6), "a time, and times, and half a time" (12:14), a short time (12:12), or "a little while" (17:10; 20:3). With the sole exception of 20:3 pointing toward the "little while" that will follow the millennium (20:7–9), all such designations refer to one identical period, the immediate crisis of the author and his readers. It is a figure lifted from the book of Daniel (Dan 7:25; 8:14; 9:27; 12:7, 11, 12), where it specified the brief time when the "abomination that desolates" was operative (Dan 8:13;

10. Jenks, *Origins of Antichrist Myth*; Peerbolte, *Antecedents of Antichrist*; Aune, *Revelation*, Excursus 13B: "The Eschatological Antagonist," 3.751–55; Lorein, *Antichrist Theme*.

9:27; 11:31; 12:11). Originally the reference was to the seizure of Jerusalem by Antiochus IV Epiphanes in 168 B.C. and his defilement of the temple with Greek sacrifices 167–164 B.C. (Dan 8:13; 11:31; 1 Macc 1:54; 2 Macc 6:2). But Jesus used the same phrase for the siege and desecration of the temple by the Romans in A.D. 70 (Matt 24:15; Mark 13:14). John, writing after the fall of Jerusalem, again re-applies the idea symbolically to an imminent desolation of God's spiritual temple, which is the church (cf. Rev 3:12; 7:15; 11:1; 21:22).

John in the 90s considered the tribulation to be incipient (1:9; 2:8–11; cf. 12:5–6). He was urgent: "Children, it is the last hour; and as you have heard that antichrist is coming, so now many antichrists have come; therefore we know that it is the last hour" (1 John 2:18). So had Paul taught a few decades earlier: "The mystery of lawlessness is already at work" (2 Thess 2:7); "in view of the present distress . . . the appointed time has grown very short" (1 Cor 7:26, 29).

THE BATTLE OF ARMAGEDDON

Though the name "Armageddon" occurs only once in the Bible (Rev 16:16),[11] the Old Testament concept of an eschatological battle of all nations allied against Israel is the model for a good number of John's visions (9:9, 16–17; 14:14–20; 16:12–16; 17:14; 19:11–21; 20:7–10). Prior prophets projected an invasion of re-inhabited Judah on the grandest scale in the future (Psa 118:10–14; Joel 3:1–16; Ezek 38–39; Zech 12:1–6; 14:1–15). Traditional Christian teaching held that Christ at his Parousia

11. Many commentators trace "Armageddon" to "Megiddo" (Judg 5:19; 2 Kings 23:29/2 Chron 35:22). See Silberman, "Armageddon"; E. H. Kline, "Why Megiddo?." But the etymology is unclear: Jauhiainen, "OT Background to Armageddon." Meredith G. Kline suggests that the name is derived from *har môʿēd*, "Mount of Assembly," with reference to Mt. Zaphon or Zion (cf. Isa 14:13; Ps 48:2): "Har Magedon."

will confront the antichrist and destroy him with the breath of his mouth (2 Thess 2:8). Armies of heaven are associated with the Parousia (e.g., Mark 8:38; 1 Thess 4:14; 2 Thess 1:7). John reflects these beliefs (Rev 19:14–15, 21).

But in the Revelation, the "battle" of Armageddon points to an intensification of the "war" the beast and his cronies have begun to wage against the church. This "war," we have seen, is essentially a scorning of Christian claims by an affluent Greco-Roman paganism in Asia loyal to the emperor, using a variety of social and legal means to bear down on Christians. The imagery borrows venerable Old Testament martial types to indicate the implacable antipathy between the Christian and the pagan world views, values, and ways of life.

We must not let the vivid descriptions of Armageddon in military terms pull us away from the stress on Christian witness that is built thematically into 19:11—20:4. To be sure, there are "iron breastplates" and "many chariots with horses running into battle" (9:9); "troops of cavalry" (9:16–17); blood flowing high as a horse's bridle (14:20); kings mustering armies for battle (16:14, 16); Christ showing up on a white horse (19:11); birds gorging themselves on the flesh of the slain (19:21). But John knew perfectly well that neither the time nor the geography of Jesus's return is predictable (Rev 3:3; 16:15; cf. Matt 24:36, 50). How, then, could he have had any illusion that the emperor would maneuver armed forces to the very place and moment of Jesus's sudden appearing in the sky (19:19)—even had the emperor been disposed to lend John's prophecies enough credence to make the attempt? All this simply cannot denote a literal battle. Otherwise no nations would survive the massacre (19:21) for the devil to deceive a thousand years later (20:7). In fact, no such barrage assailed the churches to whom John was writing (nor shall). If we stick to the preterist outlook, fruitful thus far, we should look for some fulfillment of the battle of Armageddon toward the end of the first century. History of course is eloquent that the Parousia in its fullness did not happen at that time.

Suggestive though the vocabulary might be, nothing in 19:11—20:4 entails Christ's physical coming into the world. He bears the names "faithful," "true," and "the word of God" (19:13). His weapon is a sword proceeding from his mouth (19:15, 21). His army, panoplied in fine linen (19:14) representing good deeds (19:8), fight by means of "their testimony to Jesus" and by "the word of God" (20:4; cf. 12:11). The encounter, comparable to prophetic claims that the word of God is a "fire" and a "hammer which breaks the rock in pieces" and slays its hearers (Jer 5:14; 23:29; Hos 6:5; cf. Rev 11:5–6), brings a victory of the truth about Jesus over the delusions fostered by imperial propaganda (19:20; cf. chap. 13).[12] What John refers to in 19:11–21 is prophetic, not literal warfare, dressed up in battle imagery drawn typologically from Israel's deep past.

THE QUESTION OF THE "RAPTURE"

In dispensationalist circles, the term "rapture" denotes a supernatural snatching up of believers to meet Christ in the air at his return (1 Thess 4:17; cf. Matt 24:31//Mark 13:27; Matt 24:40–41//Luke 17:34–35). This school of thought debates internally whether the rapture is to be expected at the beginning,[13] in the middle,[14] toward the end,[15] or at the very end[16] of

12. Adams, *Time at Hand*, 80–82.

13. Walvoord, *Rapture Question*. Trenchant critique of this position from a posttribulational point of view in: Gundry, *Church and Tribulation*.

14. Archer, "Mid-Seventieth Week Rapture." Critiques by Feinberg and Moo, in the same volume, pp. 147–67.

15. Rosenthal, *Pre-Wrath Rapture*; Van Kampen, *Rapture Question*. Critique from a dispensationalist perspective: Karleen, *Pre-Wrath Rapture?*

16. Gundry, *Church and Tribulation*; Kimball, *Rapture*. Riposte to Gundry from a pretribulational point of view: Walvoord, *Blessed Hope*.

the tribulation period.[17] A corollary of all views but the last is the resolution of the second coming of Christ into two: a momentary dip to remove the church from the world, then some time later a return to destroy the antichrist and set up Christ's (millennial) kingdom on earth. Those who subscribe to a pre- or a mid-tribulational rapture comfort themselves that persons who believe in Christ prior to the rapture will be spared having to go through the bitterest of persecutions. Confessors and martyrs depicted so frequently in the Apocalypse are explained to be members, not of the church, but of the Jewish people who will come to faith in Jesus after the rapture, in fulfillment of Old Testament prophecies about an end-time conversion of Israel (e.g., Isa 59:20–21; Zech 12:10—13:9).

Theories of this sort have no hoary lineage in the history of interpretation. Wholly undocumented for nearly two millennia, they originated among separatist Christians in Scotland only between 1820 and 1840,[18] and became widespread through the dissemination of the Scofield Reference Bible early in the twentieth century. They are propounded by a strident minority sector of the modern church.

That Israel and the church are two quite separate entities in God's segmented administration of history—the linchpin of

17. According to this school of thought, the tribulation is usually made out to be seven years in length, on the basis, not of any seven-year period in the book of Revelation, but of a literal interpretation of Daniel 9:27.

18. MacPherson, *Unbelievable Pre-Trib Origin*; *Incredible Cover-Up*; *Great Rapture Hoax*. Though some may find MacPherson's breezy, journalistic style hard to take seriously, his research is in fact sound. See Bruce, review of *The Unbelievable Pre-Trib Origin*. Further: Kimball, *Rapture*, 15–55. There is an unscholarly rebuttal of MacPherson in Ice, "Why not Margaret MacDonald." On pp. 162–63, for example, Ice quotes two authors as disagreeing with MacPherson, both of whose publications in fact pre-dated any of MacPherson's (Sandeen, 1970; Bell, 1967).

dispensationalism—is patently false. As we noted under the ecclesiology of the Revelation (pp. 75–76), Israel's charter as a special people (Exod 19:5–6) now belongs to the community of faith in Jesus including gentiles (Rev 1:6; 5:9–10; 7:15; cf. 1 Pet 2:9–10). Pre-christian Israelite believers and the Christian church form a continuous body (Rev 12:1–6, 13–17) moving toward a common destiny (21:12–14).[19] Suffering believers in the Apocalypse are in fact members of the church, and of no other group. A bogus dichotomy between Israel and the church, maintained in the teeth of the New Testament, is no valid canon for ruling out the pervasive evidence of a suffering church in the book of Revelation that dashes the axiom of the dispensationalist system.

Verses in the Revelation that have been offered as prooftexts for a rapture prior to the ordeal fail. "I will keep you from the hour of trial" (3:10) means that Christ will exempt his beloved ones on earth, as God kept Israel in Egypt, from the plagues that precede his coming, as shown in visionary terms by the sealing of the church before the trumpets begin (7:1–3; 9:4); "trial" refers to God's testing of the race by scourges (cf. Deut 4:34; 7:19; 29:3). "Come up hither" (4:1) invites John alone in his prophetic capacity to receive the heavenly revelations, and has nothing to do with an end-time rapture of the church. Nothing in the Apocalypse in fact corresponds to Paul's statement about believers being caught up to meet Christ. The nearest parallel describes the resurrection and ascension in a cloud of two witnesses, who signify the church (11:11–12). This event follows their becoming victims of the beast (11:7–10). Therefore the passage, such as it is, supports a post-tribulational rapture.

Indeed, the chief proof-texts outside of the Revelation for a whisking of the church away from suffering fall short. The

---

19. Hirschberg, *Eschatologische Israel*; Mayo, *Who Call Themselves Jews*.

gathering of saints of which Jesus speaks is "immediately after the tribulation of those days" (Matt 24:29//Mark 13:24). Paul's rapture, in context, coincides with "the coming (*parousia*) of the Lord" (1 Thess 4:15), of which he knows only one, namely, that to nullify the antichrist after the rebellion (2 Thess 2:1, 8). The saints will meet Christ in the air (1 Thess 4:17), not to depart the scene, but to welcome the Lord as he arrives.[20]

One of John's major aims in writing the Revelation was to nerve the church to stand firm. The decisive consideration that lies against any theory of an antecedent rapture liberating the church from the necessity of persecution is that such a view would counter the thrust of the book. Why would God address to the seven "churches" (1:4, 9) so many clarion calls to endure, if these very churches were not going to face the tribulation?

The doctrinal constructs reviewed in this section are anything but benign. They gratuitously foist upon scripture an idea wholly alien to scripture, then twist particular scriptures for warrants. They blunt the Revelation's admonishments against deception and its incitements to be faithful to the point of martyrdom. They foster an illusion that the church need not expect suffering, and create a potentially disastrous unreadiness for the crucible of the last days. They are to be refuted, so that the prophecy can summon forth courageous perseverance in Christians of the present era, as it was meant to do.

THE MILLENNIUM

Revelation 20 falls at a point where John's "Little Apocalypse" (12:1—15:4 and 19:11—21:8), having told of the tribulation, the Parousia, and the battle of Armageddon, ought to wind up, in keeping with the typical scheme of biblical eschatology, with the general resurrection, the judgment, and the establishment

20. Gundry, *Church and Tribulation*, 104–5.

of the eternal kingdom of God. Instead the account inserts an unexpected period of a thousand years. Although the kings of the earth and their armies appeared to have been wiped out at Armageddon (19:19–21), now, so that the devil can deceive "the nations" no more, an angel binds him and remands him to a bottomless pit (20:1–3). Instead of a resurrection of all the dead John sees the tribulation martyrs come to life and reign with Christ (20:4–6). Only at the end of the thousand years, after a second amassing of the heathen with Satan at their head to assault the beloved city, and their scorching defeat (20:7–10), do the resurrection, judgment, and new creation follow as expected (20:11—21:8). No hint of a parallel to this passage exists in any other cycle in chapters 6–22, nor elsewhere in the Bible.

At the center of the vision is the resurrection and co-regency with Christ of witnesses who were beheaded for their resistance to the beast, forming a climactic resolution to the theme of spiritual combat and martyrdom (2:13; 6:9–11; 13:15; 16:6; 17:6; 18:24; 19:2). Whatever else the vision might mean, it invigorates the faithful to approach martyrdom, if compelled to it, with good cheer, knowing their vindication will be swift and their honor great.

Existing Interpretations

The intrusion of a thousand-year period into the usual eschatology is perplexing, and opinions on how to understand it differ.[21]

---

21. For a cross-section of opinions, see the debate among leading proponents of four different views in Clouse, *Meaning of the Millennium*. Other dispassionate surveys: Grenz, *Millennial Maze*; Erickson, *Basic Guide to Eschatology*; Marshall, "Christian Millennium," 217–35, esp. 222–25.

Since the early second century, the two main options have been chiliasm and non-chiliasm.[22]

Chiliasm looks for the second coming of Jesus to precede the millennium, which will ensue as the final epoch of world history under the earthly rule of Christ. Hence this view is also called premillennialism. Its most widely accepted form explains the text as follows. At Armageddon, Jesus will crush the nations only partially, in spite of the universality of John's language (19:18, 21). Though the beast and the false prophet are cut off, Satan is allowed to perdure, albeit under total curtailment until a resurgence after the thousand years (20:1–3). Believers—not necessarily limited to the martyrs—will rise bodily to participate in a political monarchy of Christ over the old creation (20:4–6). When the thousand years are ended, the devil will be released and there will be a replay of something like the battle of Armageddon (20:7–10). A second resurrection will include all who died without faith in God (20:5, 12, 15).[23]

Objections to this view are formidable. How can the Parousia of Christ, which is consistently represented as the termination of evil in this world (6:15–17 with 8:1–5; 11:15–19; 14:14–20; 16:15, 17–21; 17:14; 19:1–8; cf. Matt 13:41–43; 1 Cor 15:26, 54–55; Phil 3:21; 2 Thess 1:8–9), not terminate evil for yet another thousand years? Given that resurrection is to glory (1 Cor 15), is a world still cursed a suitable habitat for the glorified (cf. Rom 8:19–23; Phil 3:21)? Why would Christ, after returning in power to found a benevolent empire, let rebellion get out of hand and sit inert with his saints in Jerusalem as

22. Hill, *Regnum Caelorum*.

23. Among the more persuasive expositions of premillennialism are Ladd, *Crucial Questions*, 133–83; *Revelation*, 259–71; "Historic Premillennialism," in Clouse, *Meaning of the Millennium*, 17–40; Bietenhard, "Millennial Hope"; *Tausendjährige Reich*; Aune, *Revelation*, 3.1069–1100, 1104–8; Osborne, *Revelation*, 696–719.

passive butts of aggression? What sort of hope for martyrs is the prospect of being besieged by diabolically inspired hordes yet a second time?

Non-chiliastic views usually see the millennium as symbolizing a present reality, setting it between Christ's first and second advents. Augustine's classic exposition includes the following points.[24] The incarceration of the dragon (20:1–3) is the binding of the strong man of which Jesus spoke during his Palestinian ministry (Mark 3:27). During the mystical thousand years, Satan's influence in the world is not eliminated, but restrained, in spite of the forcefulness of the description. He cannot stop the elect coming to faith. The thrones (Rev 20:4) represent leaders who govern the church. The first resurrection is a spiritual one, birth into eternal life when converts first come to Christ (cf. John 5:24–25). The reign with him is the influence of saints' disembodied "souls" over the world. There is no earthly monarchy of Christ, hence the unhappy tag, amillennialism.[25]

This view also faces weighty objections. Arbitrarily it posits a leap back in the narrative from what is usually taken to be the Parousia (19:11–21) to the time of Jesus's first advent, even though the start of chapter 20 falls on no structural seam, and several clauses assume narrative progress from chapter 19.[26] Does

24. Augustine, *City of God*, 20.6–14 (*NPNF*[1] 2:425–34).

25. For modern refinements of amillennialism, see Morris, *Revelation*, 233-40; Hoekema, "Amillennialism," in Clouse, *Meaning of the Millennium*, 155–87; Beale, *Revelation*, 972–1031.

26. The passage occurs in the midst of a section (19:11—21:8) consisting of units strung together by the introductory clause, "And I saw" (19:11, 17, 19; 20:1, 4, 11, 12; 21:1, 2). See Korner, "'And I Saw'"; Neall, "Amillennialism Reconsidered." The thousand years begin after the battle of Armageddon, not only in literary placement, but in narrative sequence. Some clauses in 20:1–10 refer back: "that [the dragon] should deceive the nations no more" (20:3) puts a stop to "deceived" (19:20; cf.

the passage present Satan as only relatively constrained? Do not images of Satan fettered, hurled down a bottomless shaft, and locked under a heavy cover mean complete eradication? Yet such is hardly the case during the present age (e.g., 1 Pet 5:8). To allegorize the thrones as those of ecclesiastical dignitaries, the first resurrection as the regeneration of living believers, and the reigning martyrs as departed saints, is incoherent.

A more recent non-chiliasic view takes the millennial vision as a sort of parable. The thousand years correspond to no actual period of history. Out of the story as a whole the interpreter must distill its main point. Though the martyrs suffered for a "short time," their fortunes are reversed and their reward is life—long life!—in the very environment of their former abuse. God generously overcompensates his warriers in this world for injuries in this world. An imaginary narrative thus offers encouragement to Christian witnesses.[27]

While the vision is undoubtedly encouraging, one obstacle is that everywhere in extant apocalyptic literature, a period of time stands for a period of time, even if the length can be a figurative number.[28] A more serious problem is that a fictional story presenting abstract truth does not seem to be what is needed to brace someone who is about to be tortured or executed for the faith. And this approach is inconsistent hermeneutically, in that it recognizes that John's language everywhere else is hyperbolic, yet pleads that this one scene is parabolic.

16:13–14); "who had not worshipped the beast" (20:4) defines a group antithetical to the rest of humanity "who worshipped its image" (19:20); "where the beast and the false prophet were" (20:10) refers to their having been "thrown alive into the lake of fire" (19:20).

27. This view is represented by Berkouwer, *Return of Christ*, 291–322; Bauckham, "Millennium"; McKelvey, *Millennium*.

28. D. A. Carson made this point to me in a personal conversation in the spring of 1980.

Proposal: Hyperbole Created by Reverse Typology in a Preterite Framework

Since no current interpretation of 20:1–10 is without difficulties, let us try afresh, integrating valid insights from all quarters.

With premillennialists, let us accept that the martyrs' reign lies in the future from the author's point of view. His pastoral concern is for believers of Asia who might die for their Christian profession in a romanized environment. Before their tally is complete—which it is not yet at the time of writing (6:9–11)—their "resurrection" will not take place. But John holds the rule of Christ to have begun at Christ's Ascension (1:5–6, 9; 3:21; 5:6–14; 12:5, 7–12). The tribulation is under way and the first resurrection not very far off. In the manner of Augustine, then, we can specify the focal period outlined in 20:1–10 as the era between the immediate crisis of the Asian churches in the 90s, portrayed in 19:11–21 as Armageddon, and the final manifestation of the antichrist principle at the end of history (20:7–9), the source referent of the type-images with which John clothes his current situation.

"Now" and "then" are essentially alike. An identical scheme of events happens twice in John's prophetic "diplopia."[29]

---

29. I take the term from Adams, *Time at Hand*, 17–40. I. Howard Marshall comes within a breath of this view with his "own idiosyncratic" suggestion that the millennium is "a symbol for the final state of believers" and "another picture for the heavenly kingdom" of Revelation 21–22, somewhat awkwardly duplicated and juxtaposed before the latter in keeping with the requirements of apocalyptic narrative, for reasons more compelling to John than to us. See "Christian Millennium," 227–32 [my quotes are from pp. 225, 227, 231]. He recognizes the eschatological nature of the elements that make up the millennial reign of Christ with the martyrs. But is it not more consistent with John's application of reverse typology elsewhere, particularly in chapters 12–14 (of which chapters 19–20 are the chiastic reflection), to see the millennium as describing aspects of the present age in terms of the future, rather than of the final

Release of evil powers from abyss	9:1–2; 11:7; 13:1; 17:8	20:7
Deception of the nations by antichrist	13; 16:12–16; 19:19	20:8–9a
Parousia	19:11–16	20:9b–10
Armageddon; overthrow of the ungodly	19:17–21	20:9b–10
Resurrection and judgment	20:4–5 (martyrs)	20:11–15 (general)
Presence of Christ/God	20:6 (reign with Christ)	21:1–8 (God)

A dual allusion to Ezekiel's prophecy about Gog produces an especially striking duplicity.[30]

One-thousand, a cubic number, symbolizes the time as a special one sanctified by God.[31] It will be a world-sabbath for the refreshment of the overcomers. It is not a chronological measure and does not indicate whether the time-frame will be long or short in reality (cf. Psa 90:4; 2 Pet 3:8).

The elements that make up the millennial vision are experiences that lie in the immediate future for John's readers who prove faithful, experiences graphically and hyperbolically brought close to the here and now, under forms characteristic of the age to come. Contravention of pro Roman propaganda by the prophetic witness of the church is represented as though it were the obliteration of antichrist destined to happen at the Parousia. Divine limiting of Satan is portrayed in terms of the clean sweep of the end of the

---

state under the conditions of history?

30. Both before the millennium (19:17, 21) and afterwards (20:8–9), John draws language and imagery from the same Old Testament passage, which refers to a single, eschatological event (Ezek 38–39). See Meredith G. Kline, "Har Magedon"; Bøe, *Gog and Magog*.

31. See chapter four above, pp. 56–57.

age. Entrance of the souls of martyrs into heavenly immortality is symbolized as a rising from death and an appointment to govern. In each case the present, inaugurated reality, visible only to the eye of faith, will issue in a perfect realization; the image of this future event puts its stamp on the inaugurated reality in the vision. What happens during the millennium lies beyond the present experience of John's Christian readership, but will precede the end of this present age.

On Earth or in Heaven?

Concerning the vexed question whether the millennial kingdom is located on earth or in heaven, the passage is ambiguous. Based on the variegated concept of a temporary messianic kingdom that was bandied among some Jews and Christians of John's day,[32] the description seems concrete. Yet the language, read with care, falls short of being explicit, and careful probing will show the referents to be of an ideal nature. We must distinguish between the form and the content of the vision.[33] The somewhat vague contemporary idea of an earthly reign of the messiah serves here as an apocalyptic vehicle for displaying truths that obtain during the Christian era but are by nature hidden from observation.

The millennial kingdom has a this-worldly aura. Following the carnage of Armageddon, the scene remains earthbound. Satan's binding has the terrestrial effect of preventing a mass deception of nations until he is loosed. Language of "resurrection" brings to the mind's eye the rising of bodies. Yet what the passage does not say is equally significant. The feet of the

---

32. E.g., *4 Ezra (=2 Esdras)* 7:26–44; *2 Baruch (Syriac Apocalypse)* 29–30; *Epistle of Barnabas* 15.4–9. A fuller list of relevant passages: Beasley-Murray, *Revelation*, 288–89.

33. Mounce, *Revelation*, 369–70, citing Beckwith, *Apocalypse*, 291–310, 736–38.

Word of God (19:11–21) are nowhere said to touch ground. Armageddon, interpreted, boils down to a non-military clash between the claims of Christ and those of the emperor. Whether Christ's realm is earthly or heavenly is not stated, and there is no mention of his (singular) throne. Where the martyrs enjoy their renewed vitality is left to the imagination.

For reasons advanced above in the critique of premillennialism, it is unacceptable to think of either the invincible Christ or glorified martyrs as literally present on earth to be sitting objects of the final onslaught (vv. 7–9a). Theological testing must guide us. If the triumphant christology of the entire book rules out a local presence of Christ in Jerusalem during the last invasion, then he cannot be physically on earth during the thousand years either, however evocative be the language.

Detention of the dragon in the abyss is to prevent him from raising up the final antichrist to muster an international last stand. At the level of the story his exile is unqualified, and makes for an environment in which the risen martyrs can enjoy their rest in untroubled peace. Interpreted, this earthly paradise signifies, from the point of view of martyrs' souls living secure with their Lord until the end of the age (2:10; 3:21; 6:9–11; 7:14–17; 12:12a; 14:1–5, 13; 15:2–4; 18:20), the dragon's total expulsion from the presence of the ascended Christ (12:7–12). The terrestrial idyll pictures a heavenly condition.

Certainly the image of martyrs' souls coming to life (v. 4) is bold. But it has to be symbolic, as the interpretive gloss "This resurrection is the first" (v. 5)—an instance of the formula "This is that"—requires.[34] Therefore this vivification neither refers to a corporeal event nor establishes a worldly setting for it. Its grammatical subject is the "souls of" those who have died for Christ (v. 4), as was the case in an earlier vision of martyrs pleading

34. See chapter four, pp. 52–53.

for vengeance (6:9).³⁵ The "first resurrection" is the soul's entering, during the time of this "first" creation (cf. 21:1), into a resurrection-state prior to full resurrection, a preliminary state wherein immortality has become an incontrovertible possession the "second death" cannot touch (20:6, 14).³⁶ Only by dying to this world do martyrs pass through the portal to their first resurrection; not until the age to come do they taste their second.³⁷

35. Ladd, an exponent of premillennialism, rightly notes that in New Testament usage, "come to life" and "resurrection" denote somatic resurrection by default, in the absence of contextual clues to the contrary. *Crucial Questions*, 143–49. It escapes him that Revelation 20:4 is the sole passage wherein the grammatical subject of "come to life" is disembodied "souls." This is the kind of contextual clue that can be decisive. There are others.

36. Meredith G. Kline, "First Resurrection."

37. Exegetical debate has focused too exclusively on the meaning of "came to life" and of "resurrection," and has neglected the import of "first" and "second" in this passage. On the narrative level, Henry Alford's oft-quoted remark is valid. "If, in a passage where *two resurrections* are mentioned . . . the first resurrection may be understood to mean *spiritual* rising with Christ, while the second means *literal* rising from the grave;—then there is an end of all signification in language." Henry Alford, *The Greek Testament* (Boston: Lee and Shepard, 1872) 4.732. John had a vision of bodies rising and described it as such. But what is its referent? "The vocabulary is what is because it describes a vision, not because it literally describes the referent of the vision." Poythress, "Genre and Hermeneutics," 47. We must determine the referent on other grounds. If we are willing to entertain, with premillennialists, the notion of multiple corporate resurrections in the future, a notion found nowhere in the New Testament except, allegedly, in Revelation 20:4–6, then "first" and "second" will divide the human race into separate groups of people raised on different occasions separated by a thousand-year interval. If our author subscribed to the concept of a single, general resurrection/judgment of both the righteous and the wicked, which is the ordinary teaching of the New Testament (Matthew 25:31–46; John 5:28–29; Acts 24:15)—as he in fact did (Rev 11:18; 20:12–15)—then "first" and (implied) second

Verses 4–6 denote the Church Triumphant in heaven with Christ (cf. 2:10–11, 26–28; 3:21),[38] pictured under the strong image of saints risen to share in Christ's messianic rule.

In contrast, "the camp of the saints" in verse 9 can only denote the Church Militant on earth, exposed to the devil's rage at the last (cf. 12:12).[39] If the invasion of verse 9 leads to an Armageddon that is strictly eschatological, we might have expected some mention of Christ's Parousia. But verse 9 outlines events in the sparest of terms. Omission of the Parousia is due to the fact that John has already applied the Parousia-image (19:11–21) in his (to us, preterite) context (cf. 2:5, 16, 25; 3:3, 20), and here reflects his Old Testament source, which speaks of a torrential downpour of fire and sulfur from God (Ezek 38:22).

The millennial reign, then, congruent with the nature of the throne of Christ earlier in the book (5:6–7; 12:5, 10), has repercussions both in heaven and on earth to encourage beleaguered Christians. In heaven the souls of Christian martyrs have entered into a state of life and immortality that cannot be touched by the devil or by the second death, and they reign with Christ as they await the resurrection of the body. On earth, the church catholic continues in military camp, while the devil is prevented from organizing global opposition to its witness until loosed for a final fling, to his doom.

---

will divide an individual martyr's experience of resurrection into two phases—as (implied) first and "second" plainly do in the case of death for those who accede to the beast (20:14). This nexus of "first" and "second" in reference to resurrection versus death for an individual is the crux. The resurrection-image is the sign to be interpreted; "first" and "second," as the predicates in the two narrator glosses (vv. 5, 14), do the interpreting; and both refer to individual experience of resurrection, as of death.

38. Giblin, "Millennium as Heaven."

39. On the interplay between earthly and heavenly scenes, see Gourgues, "Thousand-Year Reign."

In conclusion, Revelation 20:1–6 presents, through a pictograph of a temporary messianic kingdom on earth, reassuring implications of the enthronement and session of Christ that pertain to the intermediate state of departed Christian souls between the martyrdoms of some of John's readers and the end of the present age. If the banishment of the dragon and the resurrection of the martyrs denote facets of the invisible realm rather than of the empirical world, why would the prophecy risk confusing us by placing them in a telluric utopia? Because the goal of an apocalypse is to enable us to see what is ordinarily unseen, as the angelic chariots of fire were unveiled to Elisha's servant (2 Kings 6:17). The rational distinction between heaven and earth is deliberately blurred, things normally distributed between different spheres are presented on a single, mundane plane, to the precise end that we whose existence remains bound to the sphere of sense might apprehend the whole of reality as it truly is. The vision makes truths vivid that might not otherwise be apparent: Christ reigns supreme, his archenemy is vanquished, his martyrs live undisturbed.

Millennium and Eschatology

Revelation 19:11—20:10, then, does not modify, but adapts the simple eschatological scheme presupposed throughout the book of Revelation: troubles, antichrist and tribulation, Parousia, removal of evil from the creation, general resurrection and judgment, final kingdom of God. That sequence of events plays out both before and after the thousand years—in reverse typology at the beginning in regard to the seven churches, and afterwards, in its proper chronological context. The outline of strictly end-time events in 20:7–10 points to the natural setting of the imagery John adapts for his caricature of the exigency of the Asian churches. Here, near the end of the book, the distinction is made plain between proximate and remote eschatology.

7

Preaching and Teaching It

JOHN'S APOCALYPSE, then, has a good deal more to say about how we should live in the present, and less about the future for its own sake, than some schools of interpretation might lead us to suppose. If systems of eschatology, allegedly based upon the Revelation, can be abstruse, if predictions by Bible experts of world political developments can be sensationalist, and loyalties to cult leaders hysterical,[1] that is because it is all too easy for interpreters to magnify a fond aspect of this fascinating prophecy and lose touch with the whole, even to the point of undermining its purpose.

To teach and preach this book authoritatively, we must first appreciate it as an urgent message to churches under pressure in proconsular Asia toward the end of Domitian's reign, from which, as a word addressed by God to fellow Christians in that situation, we can extract abiding truths.[2] Churches today come under similar stresses, depending on their country, whether to participate in affluent societies, to conform to permissive behavioral standards, to trust in worldly sources of power, or to deny that Jesus is the unique Lord. In Europe and North America, Christians are increasingly marginalized by a post-Christian civilization that finds absolute truth-claims incredible and disci-

1. Nessan, "When Faith Turns Fatal."
2. Fee, "Preaching Apocalyptic?"

plined ethics obstructive. Elsewhere in the world, cases of overt maltreatment of Christians are on the rise.

Truths in the prophecy that go beyond its original occasion may be summarized in a few propositions. God is in charge. Christ is the victor over evil, now and in future. Prophecy describes reality as it is. Church and world do not mix. Present decisions have eschatological consequences. Faithfulness pays off. The future is blessed.

Let us contemplate each of these statements in turn.

GOD IS IN CHARGE

Christians in John's seven churches lived at a time when their relations with society and the state were strained. Rome, fearsome in conquest, had a practical genius for administration, engineering and commerce, and paved the way for economic benefits to accrue to lands subdued by her. Many in the cities of western Anatolia felt indebted to the proconsul at Ephesus, or to representatives of imperial power in other cities, for favors bestowed. Pagans in that part of the world showed gratitude by offering varied forms of worship to liberators, governors, or emperors. When Christians abstained from such acts on the ground that worship is due to God alone, their neighbors suspected them of ill will. The church gradually came to be ostracized and persecuted at the grass roots. John foresaw the churches' position becoming yet more dire in days to come.

When circumstances turn against us it is natural to wonder whether God's plan has gone wrong. Not only does the Revelation portray God on the throne of the universe from eternity past to eternity future, bending the course of earthly affairs to his will (1:4; 4–5); it also shows that even the nefarious designs of God's adversaries have been written into the master plan and play a necessary role in the plot. The very fact that the book allows the churches to see ahead of time the crisis of testing into which they are about to enter allays doubts about who is in control. "I have said all this to you to keep you from falling away . . . that when their hour comes you may remember that I told you of them" (John 16:1, 4).

CHRIST IS THE VICTOR OVER EVIL, NOW AND IN FUTURE

At an impasse, it is heartening to know that someone who is identified with us has himself met the enemy, absorbed the brunt of the attack, and emerged triumphant (1:17–18). Whether the kingdom of God will be successfully established in the age to come is not in doubt, for on the basis of Jesus's cross-work his kingship is inaugurated even now (5:6–14; 12:10–11). Jesus's blood has ransomed people for God (1:5; 5:9). The Lamb has engaged the adversary in the decisive battle and won it. Michael and his hosts have expelled the ancient slanderer from heaven once and for all (12:7–9). Henceforth the foe is hemmed in (12:12; 20:1–3) and there remains only a mop-up operation. And for that, the Lamb has received authorization in the form of a scroll outlining the certain destiny of the world, which he alone may open (5:1–7).

PROPHECY DESCRIBES REALITY AS IT IS

Christians, together with all partakers of urban culture in Asia, were subjected to pro-Roman brainwashing at every turn. Public buildings and art, coinage, customs required for passage through the gate of the agora, religious festivals, speeches at convocations of the municipal government, tolls at stations on the best roads, plaques of laws, heralds reporting on the armies' latest exploits—all proclaimed the might and glory of Rome.

Human beings are made for social existence. People take on a world view, a grid of subconscious assumptions by which they construe reality, largely through socialization into a culture, and from that process they cannot remain immune. While individuals may opt out of a prevailing outlook, they will not do so unless they have a reason, and even then their reaction may mirror the majority view by its very opposition.

As a prophecy, the Revelation provides an antidote to the distortions of Roman propaganda. Instead of a deified emperor it holds up a demoniac fiend (chap. 13); instead of the overflowing prosperity of the eternal city, a whore in blood-induced stupor on the brink of demise (chaps. 17–18). Jesus, regarded by Rome as a pest crucified, is shown sitting hale on his Father's throne with seraphim and countless heavenly beings falling down before him (5:8–14). His followers, thought deluded, refractory, and disloyal, are in fact priests and kings (1:6; 5:10; 7:15; 20:6; 21:9—22:5), the betrothed of the Lamb (19:7–8; 21:2, 9).

There is an implicit claim that the outlook of the Apocalypse is true, in the sense that it construes reality as God does, and cultured opinions false.

CHURCH AND WORLD DO NOT MIX

That the world was created by God is a tenet of John (Rev 4:10; 13:8; 17:8). Nevertheless he regards the world in its current state as a system steeped in the iniquity of its inhabitants and ranged against its creator. Between the will of God and the course of the world, professing Christians have to make a fateful choice. They cannot straddle the divide. Church and world are polar opposites. John's prophecy is a study in antithetical categories.

One who sits on the throne	(No counterpart; dragon's vain aspiration)
Lamb with seven horns	Beast with seven heads
Seven spirits of God	Foul spirits like frogs

Michael and his angels	Dragon and his angels
Prophets of the church	False prophet (priests of the imperial cult)
Testimony of Jesus	Obsequies to the beast
144,000 who do not worship the beast	Earth dwellers who worship the beast
Worship of God and of the Lamb	Idolatry, eating food sacrificed to idols
"Virginity" (readiness for marriage to Lamb)	"Fornication" (disqualification for marriage)
In their mouth no lie was found	Saying, "Who is like the beast?"
Suffering and martyrdom during tribulation	Rejoicing and sending gifts to one another
Protective seal against God's plagues	Agony from God's plagues
Following the Lamb wherever he goes	Gathering together at Armageddon
Trailing the rider on the white horse	Food for vultures
First resurrection until final resurrection	Death until second death
Bride of the Lamb, clad in white linen	Harlot, clad in purple and scarlet[3]
Jerusalem, forever resplendent	Babylon, forever a ruin
Eternal presence of God	Lake of fire that burns for ever and ever

To some, this either/or style of thought may seem simplistic or idealistic, perhaps a rigid outlook produced by the sour experience of a small sect on the periphery of society.[4] But it is

3. Neufeld, "Sumptuous Clothing."
4. Gager, *Kingdom and Community*, 49–57.

not because John is intellectually or temperamentally incapable of nuanced expression that he sets up antitheses, for the oracles to the churches recognize degrees of obedience and of disobedience to Christ. Rather, his analysis penetrates to the heart of the issues the church faces in the world.

PRESENT DECISIONS HAVE ESCHATOLOGICAL CONSEQUENCES

Throughout most of the Revelation, John sees the crisis in which the Asian churches are embroiled in the light of the great future. He writes as though the globe has been overtaken by the last contest between light and darkness, even though at chapter 20 he indicates that a millennium-sabbath has yet to intervene before the age ends. This seemingly exaggerated language comes to his mind, not because he is more ignorant than later generations of how far off the actual end of the world is, but to set present decisions in the light of their full significance before God.

Eschatology supplies a trove of archetypal images for the Apocalypse that have the same relation to the flow of time, as the transcendent forms or universals do in classical Greek philosophy. Even as the pure idea of a horse is embodied in the actual horse with which I am familiar, so the epic characters and events with which the age will close are instantiated in the present. The difference is that the Greeks saw the ideals as timeless, whereas John sees the antichrist, for example, as a figure of the last generation who is, in a sense, already betokened in antichrists that prefigure him.

The fusion of general eschatology with the particulars of John's day opens the door to a gamut of like applications to other particulars. John says enough to make the first-century referents of his symbols clear, but the symbols are not so specific that they cannot embrace subsequent entities as well.[5] The church ran up against the beast in the proconsuls of Asia who served Domitian, but also in Decius and Diocletian, in Stalin, Hitler, Mao, and Idi Amin. For the disappearance and re-emergence of the beast from the abyss is not only an event but a pattern that repeats itself again and again in history. Babylon the harlot was a cryptogram for the commerce of Rome, but also for the widely envied affluence of secular western Europe and North America at the beginning of the third Christian millennium. Not only has Antipas entered into his millennial reign: martyrs of every local persecution in the history of the church have joined him. The millennium may be applied as a dynamic relation, the constantly diminishing remainder of time between a progressing Now and a fixed End, already twice a thousand calendar years for the earliest martyrs, for martyrs yet to be perhaps less than a day (cf. Psa 90:4; 2 Pet 3:8)—yet for all having the quality ("1000") of a hallowed and refreshing sabbath after their labors (Rev 14:13). None of these further applications drains the symbols of their potential, nor precludes some grand fulfillment at the end of time.

In every generation, the people of God are called upon to make decisions of ultimate consequence. Individual or local eschatology is world eschatology in microcosm.

FAITHFULNESS PAYS OFF

Jesus was the pioneer of faithful witnessing in the world, and has received an everlasting kingdom with his Father. His followers having been ransomed and their robes having been washed in his blood (5:9; 7:14), the Lamb becomes the model whom they are to imitate in all things (14:4), that they too might have a stake in his "power and wealth and wisdom and might and

5. De Villiers, "Rome in Revelation."

honor and glory and blessing" (5:12). The way to salvation lies through persistent obedience.

Although the word "reward" is found but twice in the Revelation (11:18; 22:12), all the encouragements in the book presuppose a direct connection between obedience and its reward. According to the seven oracles to the churches, obtaining the promises depends on "conquering" in the specific ways indicated. These have to do with Christian speech and conduct: loving God and doing good works (2:4–5), being faithful unto death (2:10), repenting of idolatry and immorality (2:16), holding fast till Christ comes (2:25; 3:11), waking up and perfecting works (3:2–3), undergoing refinement by fire and acquiring white garments (good works, 3:18).[6]

The promises to those who conquer revolve around nothing less than eternal life: eating of the tree of life in paradise (2:7), gaining the crown that is life and being immune from the second death (2:10–11), receiving hidden manna and a white stone, symbols of the messianic feast (2:17),[7] not having one's name blotted out of the book of life (3:5), being an immovable pillar in God's temple and having the name of the new Jerusalem (3:12), sharing with Christ in his rule (2:26–28; 3:21).

These salvific rewards accrue to consistent Christian living. Those who testify to the truth in the city of this world will rise to heaven in a cloud (11:3–12). People who serve God and fear his name will have awards (11:18). Keeping the commandments of God, bearing testimony to Jesus (12:17), enduring and conquering the beast (13:10; 14:4–5, 11–13) will lead to rejoicing (15:2–4). A wedding supper is prepared for those who keep their linens pure (19:7–9). Life and authority are in store for martyrs

---

6. Homcy, "Who Overcomes."
7. Osborne, *Revelation*, 147–49.

(20:4–6). The eternal state of the saints is filled with good and satisfying things (21:9—22:5).

THE FUTURE IS BLESSED

If ever story had happy ending, it is that told in the book of Revelation. In all the promises, but especially in visions of the outcome of all things (7:15–17; 11:15–19; 19:1–9; 21:1–8; 21:9—22:5), we catch glimpses of an idyllic order, in which hunger and thirst, sunstroke and heat stroke, mourning, crying, pain, and tears are wiped away forever; in which God turns to his people and they to him in unending togetherness. This eucatastrophe is all the more poignant standing in relief against the appalling calamity that precedes it.

For some readers, however, certain things in the book cast a shadow on, rather than enhance, the goodness of God. Divine "wrath" is a prominent theme of the Apocalypse (6:16–17; 11:18; 14:10; 16:19; 19:15). Is the God who is really there characterized by wrath, or is this a projection of John's own anger onto an unworthy concept of the deity? Not only the Revelation, but the biblical canon as a whole testifies to God's resolute counteraction to anything that opposes his good counsel.[8] To say less of God would be to blur the antithesis between good and evil—to deny that the good is truly good and the evil truly evil. God's wrath is not conceived of anthropomorphically as a loss of self-control under provocation. He stores it up for the last days, giving space in the meantime for sinners to amend (cf. Rom 2:4–5).

Does the author take perhaps too morbid a delight in detailing God's final plagues and the gnawing pain they produce (chaps 8–9, 16)? No, the plagues have a purpose very much in keeping with the divine character, namely, to bring about re-

---

8. Morris, *Biblical Doctrine of Judgment*; *Apostolic Preaching*, 144–213; Campbell, "Apocalypse et Extermination."

pentance (9:20–21; 16:9, 10).[9] If their effect is rather to harden sinners in spitefulness towards God, then the horrific magnitude of the plagues becomes the measure of the high-fistedness of their human objects. It is a tribute to God's long-suffering that he goes to the utmost length, short of negating the power of self-determination he has bestowed on his creatures, to persuade his enemies of their folly in rejecting him, the only possible source of light, before he draws the curtain on their probation and encloses them in their self-chosen darkness for eternity.

Other readers wonder whether a truly good God could dish out everlasting punishment to sinners so calculatedly (14:10–11; 19:20; 20:10, 15). A partial reply is to turn the question round. How could God be truly good if impenitence and its fruits were to find a place in that permanent kingdom which is his goal? God takes no pleasure in the death of the wicked (Ezek 18:23, 32; 33:11). Retribution is strange and alien to his nature (Isa 28:21). Nothing in the Revelation suggests that he relishes this task. Indeed, he himself is not the agent who brings down the recalcitrant: he so directs the rage of his foes that the kingdom of evil will self-destruct (17:16–17). The lake of fire is not a torment vindictively superadded to the incorrigibility of some, but a symbol of what that choice itself entails. In a monotheistic universe, where there is but one ontological ground of all goodness, to decline that ground is to decline with it any and every comfort.

Lastly, some are troubled by the motif of divine vengeance for the cause of the martyrs (6:10; 19:2). Is this a sub-christian sentiment, in comparison with the noble prayers of Jesus and of certain Christians that God might forgive the artificers of their wrongs and forego avenging them (Luke 23:34; Acts 7:60; 2 Tim 4:16)? The symbolic vignette in 6:9–11 is not held up as a psychology of victimization to emulate, but points objectively to

9. Aune, *Revelation*, 2.416–19.

the law of recompense for injuries in a moral universe.[10] God is there to guarantee that the rights of the downtrodden cannot be trampled by the will of the unjust without redress. Should they themselves wish voluntarily to renounce vengeance, nothing in the Revelation forbids that.

In the Apocalypse, John depicts the climax of the ages-long duel between good and evil, and its predetermined result, the ascendancy of the dream of the unblemished God. The prophet affirms the genuine antithesis of the evil to the good within the unicity of the comprehensive divine will. He skillfully avoids, on the one side, a monism in which good and evil would be but mutually relative manifestations of one metaphysical principle, neither wholly opposed to the other. On the other hand, he steers clear of a dualism in which good and evil would be opposite poles counterbalancing each other in aeonic tension. The conflict is fierce, the antagonism real and titanic. But it takes place under One who sits on the throne, who was there before it began, who will be there when it is over—to share with those who conquer with him the unending joy of the Almighty and the Lamb who share the Spirit.

---

10. Ritt, "Rachphantasie?"

Bibliography

Adams, Jay E. *The Time Is at Hand*. Phillipsburg, NJ: Presbyterian and Reformed, 1966.

Aharoni, Yohanan, and Michael Avi-Yonah. *The Macmillan Bible Atlas*. Rev. ed. New York: Macmillan, 1977.

Anchor Bible Dictionary. Edited by David Noel Freedman. 6 vols. New York: Doubleday, 1992.

Ante-Nicene Fathers. Edited by Alexander Roberts, et al. 10 vols. 1885–1897. Repr. Peabody, MA: Hendrickson, 1994.

Apuleius. *The Golden Ass*. Translated and edited by Jack Lindsay. Indiana University Greek and Latin Classics. Bloomington, IN: University of Indiana Press, 1962.

Archer, Gleason L. "The Case for the Mid-Seventieth-Week Rapture Position." In *The Rapture Question: Pre-, Mid-, or Post-Tribulational?*, introduced by Richard R. Reiter, 113–45. Grand Rapids: Zondervan, 1984.

Aune, David. E. "The Apocalypse of John and Palestinian Jewish Apocalyptic." *Neot* 40 (2006) 1–33.

———. *Revelation*. 3 vols. WBC, 52A–C. Dallas: Word, 1997–1998.

Bacchiocchi, Samuele. *Hal Lindsey's Prophetic Jigsaw Puzzle: Five Predictions That Failed*. Berrien Springs, MI: Biblical Perspectives, 1987.

Backus, I. *Reformation Readings of the Apocalypse: Geneva, Zurich, and Wittenberg*. Oxford Studies in Historical Theology. Oxford: Oxford University Press, 2000.

Barnett, Paul. "Polemical Parallelism: Some Further Reflections on the Apocalypse." *JSNT* 35 (1989) 111–20.

Barr, D. L., ed. *Reading the Book of Revelation: A Resource for Students*. SBLRBS, 44. Atlanta: Society of Biblical Literature, 2003.

Bass, Clarence B. *Backgrounds to Dispensationalism: Its Historical Genesis and Ecclesiastical Implications*. Grand Rapids: Eerdmans, 1960.

Bauckham, Richard. *The Climax of Prophecy: Studies on the Book of Revelation*. Edinburgh: T&T Clark, 1993.

———. "The List of the Tribes in Revelation 7 Again." *JSNT* 42 (1991) 99–115.

———. "The Millennium." In *God Will Be All in All: The Eschatology of Jürgen Moltmann*, edited by Richard Bauckham, 123–47. Edinburgh: T & T Clark, 1999.

———. *The Theology of the Book of Revelation*. New Testament Theology. Cambridge: Cambridge University Press, 1993.

Beale, G. K. *The Book of Revelation: A Commentary on the Greek Text*. NIGTC. Grand Rapids: Eerdmans, 1999.

———. *John's Use of the Old Testament in Revelation*. JSNTSup, 166. Sheffield: Sheffield Academic Press, 1998.

———. "The Purpose of Symbolism in the Book of Revelation." *CTJ* 41 (2006) 53–66.

Beasley-Murray, G. R. *The Book of Revelation*. Rev. ed. NCB. London: Marshall, Morgan and Scott, 1978.

Beckwith, Isbon T. *The Apocalypse of John*. New York: Macmillan, 1919.

Bell, Albert A. "The Date of John's Apocalypse. The Evidence of Some Roman Historians Reconsidered." *NTS* 25 (1978/1979) 93–102.

Ben-Daniel, J., and G. Ben Daniel. *The Apocalypse in the Light of the Temple: A New Approach to the Book of Revelation*. Jerusalem: Beit Yochanan, 2003.

Berkouwer, G. C. *The Return of Christ*. Edited by Marlin J. Van Elderen. Translated by James Van Oosterom. Studies in Dogmatics. Grand Rapids: Eerdmans, 1972.

Bietenhard, Hans. "The Millennial Hope in the Early Church." *SJT* 6 (1953) 12–30.

———. *Das tausendjährige Reich: Eine biblisch-theologische Studie*. Zürich: Zwingli, 1955.

Biguzzi, G. "Is the Babylon of Revelation Rome or Jerusalem?" *Bib* 87 (2006) 371–86.

Böcher, O. *Die Johannesapokalypse*. 4th ed. EdF, 41. Darmstadt: Wissenschaftliche Buchgesellschaft, 1998.

Bøe, Sverre. *Gog and Magog: Ezekiel 38–39 as Pre-Text for Revelation 19,17–21 and 20,7–10*. WUNT, 2/135. Tübingen: Mohr Siebeck, 2001.

Böttrich, C. "Das 'gläserne Meer' in Apk 4,6/15,2." *BN* 80 (1995) 5–15.

Briggs, Robert A. *Jewish Temple Imagery in the Book of Revelation*. Studies in Biblical Literature, 10. New York: Peter Lang, 1999.

Bruce, F. F. *New Testament History*. Anchor Books. Garden City, NY: Doubleday, 1972.

———. Review of *The Unbelievable Pre-Trib Origin*, by Dave MacPherson. *EvQ* 47 (1975) 58.

Buby, B. A. "The Fascinating Woman of Revelation 12." *Marian Studies* 50 (1999) 107–26.

———. *A Journey through Revelation: A Message for the New Millennium*. New York: Alba House, 2000.

Busch, Peter. *Der gefallene Drache: Mythenexegese am Beispiel von Apokalypse 12*. Texte und Arbeiten zum neutestamentlichen Zeitalter, 19. Tübingen: Francke, 1996.

Caird, G. B. *The Language and Imagery of the Bible*. Philadelphia: Westminster, 1980.

Calder, William M., and John M. Cook. "Ephesus." In *OCD²*, 387.

Callahan, A. D. "Apocalypse as Critique of Political Economy: Some Notes on Revelation 18." *HBT* 21 (1999) 46–65.

Campbell, G. "Antithetical Feminine-Urban Imagery and a Tale of Two Women-Cities in the Book of Revelation." *TynBul* 55 (2004) 81–108.

Campbell, W. G. "Apocalypse et extermination." *RRef* 54 (2003) 89–107.

———. "Apocalypse johannique et persévérance des saints." *RRef* 57 (2006) 43–55.

Carcopino, Jérôme. *Daily Life in Ancient Rome: The People and the City at the Height of the Empire*. Edited by Henry T. Rowell. Translated by E. O. Lorimer. New Haven: Yale University Press, 1940.

Carrell, P. R. *Jesus and the Angels: Angelology and the Christology of the Apocalypse of John*. SNTSMS, 95. Cambridge: Cambridge University Press, 1997.

Charles, R. H. *A Critical and Exegetical Commentary on the Revelation of St. John*. ICC. New York: Scribner, 1920.

Clouse, Robert G., ed. *The Meaning of the Millennium: Four Views*. Downers Grove, IL: InterVarsity, 1977.

Collins, Adela Yarbro. *The Combat Myth in the Book of Revelation*. HDR, 9. Missoula, MT: Scholars, 1976.

———. *Crisis and Catharsis: The Power of the Apocalypse*. Philadelphia: Westminster, 1984.

Couch, M., ed. *A Bible Handbook to Revelation*. Grand Rapids: Kregel, 2001.

Court, John M. *Revelation*. NTG. Sheffield: JSOT Press, 1994.

Dalrymple, R. "These Are the Ones . . . (Rev 7)." *Bib* 86 (2005) 396–406.

Davis, William Stearns. *The Influence of Wealth in Imperial Rome*. New York: Macmillan, 1910.

De Groote, M. "Die Johannesapokalypse und die Kanonbildung im Osten." *ZKT* 116 (2005) 147–60.

———. "Kanonbildung im Westen: Das Schicksal der Johannesapokalypse." *ZKG* 114 (2003) 323–32.

De Smidt, K. "The Acts of God and the Spirit in the Church(es) and in the World: A Meta-Theology of o(qeo&j and to_ pneu-ma in Revelation 1:4." *Acta Patristica et Byzantina* 16 (2005) 166–95.

———. "A Meta-Theology of o(qeo&j in Revelation 1:1–2." *Neot* 38 (2004) 183–208.

De Villiers, P. G. R. "Persecution in the Book of Revelation." *AcT* 22 (2002) 47–70.

———. "The Role of Composition in the Interpretation of the Rider on the White Horse and the Seven Seals in Revelation." *Hervormde Teologiese Studies* 60 (2004) 125–53.

———. "Rome in the Historical Interpretation of Revelation." *Acta Patristica et Byzantina* 13 (2002) 120–42.

Decock, P. B. "The Scriptures in the Book of Revelation." *Neot* 33 (1999) 373–410.

DeSilva, D. A. "The Construction and Social Function of a Counter-Cosmos in the Revelation of John." *Forum* 9 (1993) 47–61.

Desrosiers, G. *An Introduction to Revelation*. Continuum Biblical Studies. London: Continuum, 2000.

Dio Cassius. Translated by Earnest Cary. 9 vols. Loeb Classical Library. Cambridge, MA: Harvard University Press, 1914–1927.

Dochhorn, J. "Und die Erde tat ihren Mund auf: Ein Exodusmotive in Apc 12,16." *ZNW* 88 (1997) 140–42.

Dudley, Donald R. *The Civilization of Rome*. London: New English Library, 1962.

Dumbrell, William J. *The End of the Beginning: Revelation 21–22 and the Old Testament*. Moore Theological College Lecture Series. Grand Rapids: Baker, 1985.

Easley, K. *Living with the End in Sight*. Nashville: Holman, 2000.

Edson, Charles F. "Ruler-Cult. I. Greek." In *OCD*[2], 938–39.

Encyclopedia of the Early Church. Edited by Angelo Di Berardino. Prepared by Istituto patristico Augustinianum. Translated by Adrian Walford. Foreword by W. H. C. Frend. 2 vols. New York: Oxford University Press, 1992.

Erickson, Millard J. *A Basic Guide to Eschatology: Making Sense of the Millennium*. Grand Rapids: Baker, 1998.

———. *Contemporary Options in Eschatology: A Study of the Millennium*. Grand Rapids: Baker, 1977.

Eusebius. *The Ecclesiastical History*. Translated by Kirsopp Lake and J. E. L. Oulton. Loeb Classical Library. 2 vols. London: Heinemann, 1926–1932.

Faley, R. J. *Apocalypse Then and Now: A Companion to the Book of Revelation*. New York: Paulist, 1999.

Fee, Gordon D. "Preaching Apocalyptic? You've Got to Be Kidding!" *CTJ* 41 (2006) 7–16.

Fekkes, Jan. *Isaiah and Prophetic Traditions in the Book of Revelation: Visionary Antecedents and Their Development*. JSNTSup, 93. Sheffield: JSOT Press, 1994.

Ferguson, Everett. *Backgrounds of Early Christianity*. Grand Rapids: Eerdmans, 1987.

Fiensy, David A. "The Roman Empire and Asia Minor." In *The Face of New Testament Studies: A Survey of Recent Research*, edited by Scot McKnight and Grant Osborne, 36–56. Grand Rapids: Baker, 2004.

Filho, J. A. "The Apocalypse of John as an Account of a Visionary Experience." *JSNT* 25 (2002) 213–34.

Fiorenza, Elisabeth Schüssler. *The Book of Revelation: Justice and Judgment*. Philadelphia: Fortress, 1985.

———. *Revelation: Vision of a Just World*. Edinburgh: T&T Clark, 1993.

Fishwick, Duncan. *The Imperial Cult in the Latin West: Studies in the Ruler Cult of the Western Provinces of the Roman Empire*. EPRO, 108. Leiden: Brill, 1987.

Flegg, C. G. *An Introduction to Reading the Apocalypse*. Crestwood, NY: St. Vladimir's Seminary Press, 1999.

Frankfurter, David. "Jews or Not? Reconstructing the 'Other' in Rev 2:9 and 3:9." *HTR* 94 (2001) 403–25.

Franz, G. "Propaganda, Power, and the Perversion of Biblical Truths: Coins Illustrating the Book of Revelation." *Bible and Spade* 19 (2006) 73–87.

Friesen, Steven J. "Asia Minor's Provincial Cult in Ephesus and the Interpretation of the Book of Revelation." Paper presented at the annual meeting of the SBL. New Orleans, November 18,1990.

———. *Imperial Cults and the Apocalypse of John: Reading Revelation in the Ruins*. Oxford: Oxford University Press, 2001.

———. "Myth and Symbolic Resistance in Revelation 13." *JBL* 123 (2004) 281–313.

———. *Twice Neokoros: Ephesus, Asia, and the Cult of the Flavian Imperial Family*. Religions in the Graeco-Roman World, 116. Leiden: Brill, 1993.

Frykholm, Amy Johnson. *Rapture Culture: Left Behind in Evangelical America*. Oxford: Oxford University Press, 2004.

Gager, John G. *Kingdom and Community: The Social World of Early Christianity*. Prentice-Hall Studies in Religion. Englewood Cliffs, NJ: Prentice-Hall, 1975.

Garnsey, Peter, and Richard Saller. *The Roman Empire: Economy, Society and Culture*. Berkeley: University of California Press, 1987.

Gerstner, John H. *Wrongly Dividing the Word of Truth: A Critique of Dispensationalism*. Brentwood, TN: Wolgemuth & Hyatt, 1991.

Giblin, C. H. "The Millennium (Rev 20.4–6) as Heaven." *NTS* 45 (1999) 553–70.

Gilbertson, Michael. *God and History in the Book of Revelation: New Testament Studies in Dialogue with Pannenberg and Moltmann*. SNTSMS, 124. Cambridge: Cambridge University Press, 2003.

Glasson, T. Francis. "The Temporary Messianic Kingdom and the Kingdom of God." *JTS* 41 (1990) 517–25.

Glonner, Georg. *Zur Bildersprache des Johannes von Patmos: Untersuchung der Johannesapokalypse anhand einer um Elemente der Bildinterpretation erweiterten historisch-kritischen Methode*. NTAbh, 34. Münster: Aschendorff, 1999.

González, J. L. *For the Healing of the Nations: The Book of Revelation in an Age of Cultural Conflict*. Maryknoll, NY: Orbis, 1999.

Gourgues, M. "The Thousand-Year Reign (Rev 20:1–6): Terrestrial or Celestial?" *CBQ* 47 (1985) 676–81.

Grelot, P. "Marie Mère de Jésus dans les Écritures." *NRTh* 121 (1999) 59–71.

Grenz, Stanley J. *The Millennial Maze: Sorting Out Evangelical Options*. Downers Grove, IL: InterVarsity, 1992.

Gundry, Robert H. *The Church and the Tribulation: A Biblical Examination of Posttribulationism*. Contemporary Evangelical Perspectives. Grand Rapids: Zondervan, 1973.

Hall, John F. "Rome." In *ABD* 5:830–34.

Hall, Mark Seaborn. "The Hook Interlocking Structure of Revelation: The Most Important Verses in the Book and How They May Unify Its Structure." *NovT* 44 (2002) 278–96.

Hammond, Mason. "Ruler-Cult. II. Roman." *OCD*², 939–40.

Hanna, K. F. A. *La passione di Cristo nell'Apocalisse*. Tesi Gregoriana, Serie Teologia, 77. Rome: Editrice Pontificia Università Gregoriana, 2001.

Hannah, Darrell D. "Of Cherubim and the Divine Throne: Rev 5.6 in Context." *NTS* 49 (2003) 528–42.

---------. "The Throne of His Glory: The Divine Throne and Heavenly Mediators in Revelation and the Similitudes of Enoch." *ZNW* 94 (2003) 68–96.

Hanson, Paul D. *The Dawn of Apocalyptic*. Philadelphia: Fortress, 1975.

Harland, Philip A. "Honouring the Emperor or Assailing the Beast: Participation in Civic Life among Associations (Jewish, Christian and Other) in Asia Minor and the Apocalypse of John." *JSNT* 77 (2000) 99–121.

Heike, T., and T. Nicklas. *"Die Worte der Prophetie dieses Buches": Offenbarung 22, 6–21 als Schlussstein der christlichen Bibel Alten und Neuen Testaments gelesen*. Biblisch-Theologische Studien, 62. Neukirchen-Vluyn: Neukirchner, 2003.

Hemer, Colin J. *The Letters to the Seven Churches of Asia in Their Local Setting*. JSNTSup, 11. Sheffield: JSOT Press, 1986.

Hendriksen, William. *More Than Conquerors: An Interpretation of the Book of Revelation*. 6th ed. Grand Rapids: Baker, 1952.

Hengel, Martin. "Die Throngemeinschaft des Lammes mit Gott in der Johannesapokalypse." *TBei* 27 (1996) 159–75.

Hennecke, Edgar. *New Testament Apocrypha*. Edited by Wilhelm Schneemelcher. Translated and edited by R. McL. Wilson. 2 vols. Philadelphia: Westminster, 1963.

Herms, R. *An Apocalypse for the Church and for the World: The Narrative Function of Universal Language in the Book of Revelation*. BZNW, 143. Berlin: De Gruyter, 2006.

Hill, Charles E. *The Johannine Corpus in the Early Church*. Oxford: Oxford University Press, 2004.

---------. *Regnum Caelorum: Patterns of Future Hope in Early Christianity*. Oxford Early Christian Studies. Oxford: Clarendon, 1992.

Hirschberg, P. *Das eschatologische Israel: Untersuchungen zum Gottesvolkverständnis der Johannesoffenbarung*. WMANT, 84. Neukirchen-Vluyn: Neukirchener, 1999.

Hoekema, Anthony A. *The Bible and the Future*. Grand Rapids: Eerdmans, 1979.

Hoffmann, M. R. *The Destroyer and the Lamb: The Relationship between Angelomorphic and Lamb Christology in the Book of Revelation*. WUNT, 2/203. Tübingen: Mohr Siebeck, 2005.

Hofius, O. "7)Arni/on—Widder oder Lamm? Erwägungen zur Bedeutung des Wortes in der Johannesapokalypse." *ZNW* 89 (1998) 272–81.

Homcy, S. L. "'To Him Who Overcomes': A Fresh Look at What 'Victory' Means for the Believer according to the Book of Revelation." *JETS* 38 (1995) 193–201.

Horace. *The Odes and Epodes*. Translated by C. E. Bennett. Loeb Classical Library. Cambridge, MA: Harvard University Press, 1914.

Howard-Brook, W., and A. Gwyther. *Unveiling Empire: Reading Revelation Then and Now*. Bible and Liberation. Maryknoll, NY: Orbis, 1999.

Ice, Thomas D. "Why the Doctrine of the Pretribulational Rapture Did Not Begin with Margaret MacDonald." *BSac* 147 (1990) 155–68.

Irenaeus. *Against Heresies*. In *ANCF* 1:307–567.

Jauhiainen, Marko. *The Use of Zechariah in Revelation*. WUNT, 2/199. Tübingen: Mohr Siebeck, 2005.

———. "The OT Background to *Armageddon* (Rev. 16:16 Revisited)." *NovT* 47 (2005) 381–93.

———. "Recapitulation and Chronological Progression in John's Apocalypse: Towards a New Perspective." *NTS* 49 (2003) 543–59.

Jenks, G. C. *The Origins and Early Development of the Antichrist Myth*. BZNW, 59. Berlin: De Gruyter, 1991.

Josephus. Translated by H. St. J. Thackeray, et al. 10 vols. Loeb Classical Library. Cambridge, MA: Harvard University Press, 1926–1965.

Judge, Edwin A. "The Mark of the Beast, Revelation 13:16." *TynBul* 42 (1991) 158–60.

Kaiser, Walter C. *Toward an Old Testament Theology*. Grand Rapids: Zondervan, 1978.

Karleen, Paul S. *The Pre-Wrath Rapture of the Church: Is It Biblical?* Langhorne, PA: BF Press, 1991.

Kellerman, J. A. "Why One Thousand Years?" *Concordia Journal* 31 (2005) 140–49.

Kimball, William R. *The Rapture: A Question of Timing*. Grand Rapids: Baker, 1985.

Klauck, Hans-Josef. "Do They Never Come Back? *Nero Redivivus* and the Apocalypse of John." *CBQ* 63 (2001) 683–98.

Kline, E. H. "Why Megiddo?" *BRev* 16 (2000) 22–31, 46.

Kline, Meredith G. "The First Resurrection." *WTJ* 37 (1974–1905) 366–75.

———. "Har Magedon: The End of the Millennium." *JETS* 39 (1996) 207–22.

Knight, J. *Revelation*. Readings: A New Biblical Commentary. Sheffield: Sheffield Academic Press, 1999.

Koester, Craig R. *Revelation and the End of All Things*. Grand Rapids: Eerdmans, 2001.

———. "Revelation and the *Left Behind* Novels." *WW* 25 (2005) 274–82.

Korner, Ralph J. "'And I Saw . . .': An Apocalyptic Literary Convention for Structural Identification in the Apocalypse." *NovT* 42 (2000) 160–83.

Kovacs, J., and C. Rowland. *Revelation*. Blackwell Bible Commentaries. Oxford: Blackwell, 2003.

Kowalski, B. *Die Rezeption des Propheten Ezechiel in der Offenbarung des Johannes*. SBB, 52. Stuttgart: Katholisches Bibelwerk, 2004.

Kramer, H. W. "Contrast as a Key to Understanding *The Revelation to St. John*." *Concordia Journal* 23 (1997) 108–17.

Kraybill, J. N. *Imperial Cult and Commerce in John's Apocalypse*. JSNTSup, 132. Sheffield: Sheffield Academic Press, 1996.

Kyrtatas, D. J. "The Apocalypse: Revelation and Prophecy." *TBT* 34 (1996) 353–58.

Ladd, George E. *A Commentary on the Revelation of John*. Grand Rapids: Eerdmans, 1972.

———. *Crucial Questions about the Kingdom of God*. Grand Rapids: Eerdmans, 1952.

LaHaye, Tim, and Jerry Jenkins. *Left Behind: A Novel of Earth's Last Days*. Wheaton, IL: Tyndale House, 1995.

Lambrecht, J. "Jewish Slander: A Note on Revelation 2,9–10." *ETL* 75 (1999) 421–29.

Langdon, M. K. "Classifying the Hills of Rome." *Eranos* 97 (1999) 98–107.

Le Moignan, C. *Following the Lamb: A Reading of Revelation for the New Millennium*. London: Epworth, 2000.

Lee, D. *The Narrative Asides in the Book of Revelation*. Lanham: University Press of America, 2002.

Lee, P. *The New Jerusalem in the Book of Revelation: A Study of Revelation 21–22 in the Light of Its Background in Jewish Tradition*. WUNT, 2/129. Tübingen: Mohr Siebeck, 2001.

Lindsey, Hal. *The Late Great Planet Earth*. Grand Rapids: Zondervan, 1970.

Lioy, D. *The Book of Revelation in Christological Focus*. Studies in Biblical Literature, 58. New York: Lang, 2003.

Longenecker, Bruce W. "'Linked Like a Chain': Rev 22.6–9 in Light of an Ancient Transition Technique." *NTS* 47 (2001) 105–17.

Lorein, G. W. *The Antichrist Theme in the Intertestamental Period*. JSPSup, 44. London: T & T Clark, 2003.

Lucian. Translated by A. M. Harmon, et al. 8 vols. Loeb Classical Library. Cambridge, MA: Harvard University Press, 1913–1967.

Lumsden, D. W. *And Then the End Will Come: Early Latin Christian Interpretations of the Opening of the Seven Seals*. Medieval History and Culture. New York: Garland, 2001.

Maahs, K. H. *Of Angels, Beasts, and Plagues: The Message of Revelation for a New Millennium*. Valley Forge, PA: Judson, 1999.

McDonough, Sean M. *YHWH at Patmos: Rev. 1:4 in Its Hellenistic and Early Jewish Setting*. WUNT, 2/107. Tübingen: Mohr Siebeck, 1999.

McIlraith, D. A. "'For the Fine Linen is the Righteous Deeds of the Saints': Works and Wife in Revelation 19:8." *CBQ* 61 (1999) 512–29.

McKelvey, R. J. "Jews in the Book of Revelation." *IBS* 25 (2003) 175–94.

———. *The Millennium and the Book of Revelation*. Cambridge: Lutterworth, 1999.

MacPherson, Dave. *The Great Rapture Hoax*. Fletcher, NC: New Puritan Library, 1983.

———. *The Incredible Cover-up: The True Story on the Pre-Trib Rapture*. Plainfield, NJ: Logos, 1975.

———. *The Unbelievable Pre-Trib Origin: The Recent Discovery of a Well-Known Theory's Beginning, and Its Incredible Cover-Up*. Kansas City, MO: Heart of America Bible Society, 1973.

McRay, John. *Archaeology and the New Testament*. Grand Rapids: Baker, 1991.

Maier, H. O. *Apocalypse Recalled: The Book of Revelation after Christendom*. Minneapolis: Fortress, 2002.

Marcato, G. "Carisma profetico e autorità apostolica nell'Apocalisse." *Ang* 79 (2002) 5–18.

Martial. Translated by Walter C. A. Ker. Loeb Classical Library. 2 vols. Cambridge, MA: Harvard University Press, 1919–1920.

Marshall, I. H. "The Christian Millennium." *EvQ* 72 (2000) 217–35.

Marucci, C. "Gematrie und Isopsephie im Neuen Testament: Eine wirkliche Hilfe zum Verständnis?" SNTSU 27 (2002) 179–97.

Massyngberde Ford, J. *Revelation*. AB, 38. Garden City, NY: Doubleday, 1975.

Mathewson, David. "The Destiny of the Nations in Revelation 21:1—22:5: A Reconsideration." *TynBul* 53 (2002) 121–42.

———. *A New Heaven and a New Earth: The Meaning and Function of the Old Testament in Revelation 21.1—22.5*. JSNTSup, 238. London: Sheffield Academic Press, 2003.

Mayo, Philip L. *"Those Who Call Themselves Jews": The Church and Judaism in the Apocalypse of John.* Princeton Theological Monograph Series, 60. Eugene, OR: Pickwick, 2006.

———. "The Role of the *Birkath Haminim* in Early Jewish-Christian Relations: A Reexamination of the Evidence." *BBR* 16 (2006) 325–43.

Mealy, J. Webb. *After the Thousand Years: Resurrection and Judgment in Revelation 20.* JSNTSup, 70. Sheffield: JSOT Press, 1992.

Metzger, Bruce M. *Breaking the Code: Understanding the Book of Revelation.* Nashville: Abingdon, 1993.

Michaels, J. Ramsey. *Interpreting the Book of Revelation.* Guides to New Testament Exegesis, 7. Grand Rapids: Baker, 1992.

———. "Revelation 1.19 and the Narrative Voices of the Apocalypse." *NTS* 37 (1991) 604–20.

Moore, A. L. *The Parousia in the New Testament.* NovTSup, 13. Leiden: Brill, 1966.

Morris, Leon. *The Apostolic Preaching of the Cross.* 3rd ed. Grand Rapids: Eerdmans, 1965.

———. *The Biblical Doctrine of Judgment.* London: Tyndale, 1960.

———. *The Revelation of St. John.* TNTC. Grand Rapids: Eerdmans, 1969.

Morton, Russell. "Glory to God and to the Lamb: John's Use of Jewish and Hellenistic/Roman Themes in Formatting His Theology in Revelation 4–5." *JSNT* 83 (2001) 89–109.

Mounce, Robert H. *The Book of Revelation.* NICNT. Grand Rapids: Eerdmans, 1998.

Moyise, S. "Does the Author of Revelation Misappropriate the Scriptures?" *AUSS* 40 (2002) 3–21.

———. "Intertextuality and the Use of Scripture in the Book of Revelation." *Scriptura* 84 (2003) 391–401.

———. *The Old Testament in the Book of Revelation.* JSNTSup, 115. Sheffield: Sheffield Academic Press, 1995.

———. "The Old Testament in the New: A Reply to Greg Beale." *IBS* 21 (1999) 54–58.

———. "Singing the Song of Moses and the Lamb: John's Dialogical Use of Scripture." *AUSS* 42 (2004) 347–60.

Neall, B. S. "Amillennialism Reconsidered." *AUSS* 43 (2005) 185–210.

Nessan, C. L. "When Faith Turns Fatal: David Koresh and Tragic Misreadings of Revelation." *CurTM* 22 (1995) 191–99.

Neufeld, D. "Sumptuous Clothing and Ornamentation in the Apocalypse." *HvTSt* 58 (2002) 664–89.

New International Dictionary of New Testament Theology. Edited by Colin Brown. 3 vols. Grand Rapids: Zondervan, 1975–78.

Newman, B. "The Fallacy of the Domitian Hypothesis: Critique of the Irenaeus Source as a Witness for the Contemporary-Historical Approach to the Interpretation of the Apocalypse." *NTS* 10 (1963–1964) 133–39.

Newport, K. G. C. *Apocalypse and Millennium: Studies in Biblical Eisegesis*. Cambridge: Cambridge University Press, 2000.

Nicene and Post-Nicene Fathers: First Series. Edited by Philip Schaff. 14 vols. 1886–1889. Repr. Peabody, MA: Hendrickson, 1994.

Nicene and Post-Nicene Fathers: Second Series. Edited by Philip Schaff and Henry Wace. 14 vols. 1890–1900. Repr. Peabody, MA: Hendrickson, 1994.

Noē, J. "An Exegetical Basis for a Preterist-Idealist Understanding of the Book of Revelation." *JETS* 49 (2006) 767–96.

Nwachukwu, O. O. *Beyond Vengeance and Protest: A Reflection on the Macarisms in Revelation*. Studies in Biblical Literature, 71. New York: Lang, 2004.

Osborne, Grant R. *Revelation*. BECNT, 19. Grand Rapids: Baker Academic, 2002.

Osiek, C. "Apocalyptic Eschatology." *TBT* 34 (1996) 341–45.

Oster, Richard E. "Ephesus (Place)." *ABD* 2:542–49.

Oxford Classical Dictionary. 2nd ed. Edited by N. G. L. Hammond and H. H. Scullard. Oxford: Clarendon, 1970.

Pate, C. Marvin. *Four Views on the Book of Revelation*. Grand Rapids: Zondervan, 1998.

Peerbolte, L. J. Lietaert. *The Antecedents of Antichrist: A Traditio-Historical Study of the Earliest Christian Views on Eschatological Opponents*. JSJSup, 49. Leiden: Brill, 1996.

Pender, W. C. *Revelation*. Interpretation Bible Studies. Louisville: Westminster John Knox, 1999.

Pentecost, J. Dwight. *Things to Come: A Study in Biblical Eschatology*. Grand Rapids: Zondervan, 1964.

Petronius. *The Satyricon*. Translated and edited by William Arrowsmith. New York: New American Library, 1959.

Pisano, O. *La radice e la stirpe di David: salmi davidici nel libro dell'Apocalisse*. Tesi Gregoriana, Serie Teologia, 85. Rome: Editrice Pontificia Università Gregoriana, 2002.

Pliny. *Letters and Panegyricus*. Translated by Betty Radice. 2 vols. Loeb Classical Library. Cambridge, MA: Harvard University Press, 1969.

Porter, Stanley E. "The Language of the Apocalypse in Recent Discussion." *NTS* 35 (1989) 582–603.

Poythress, Vern Sheridan "Counterfeiting in the Book of Revelation as a Perspective on Non-Christian Culture." *JETS* 40 (1997) 411–18.

———. "Genre and Hermeneutics in Rev 20:1–6." *JETS* 36 (1993) 41–54.

Price, S. R. F. *Rituals and Power: The Roman Imperial Cult in Asia Minor.* Cambridge: Cambridge University Press, 1984.

Pritchard, James B., ed. *Ancient Near Eastern Texts Relating to the Old Testament.* 3d ed. Princeton: Princeton University Press, 1969.

Rainbow, Paul A. "Millennium as Metaphor in John's Apocalypse." *WTJ* 58 (1996) 209–21.

Ramsay, William M. *The Letters to the Seven Churches of Asia.* Updated ed. Peabody, MA: Hendrickson, 1994.

Richmond, Ian A., and Ferdinando Castagnoli. "Rome (Topography)." In *OCD*^{2}, 935–36.

Riley, W. "Who Is the Woman of Revelation 12?" *PIBA* 18 (1995) 15–39.

Ritt, H. "Rachphantasie, infantiles Weltbild, psychischer Konflikt? Gewalt in der Offenbarung des Johannes." *BK* 51 (1996) 128–32.

Rosenthal, Marvin. *The Pre-Wrath Rapture of the Church: A New Understanding of the Rapture, the Tribulation, and the Second Coming.* Nashville: Thomas Nelson, 1990.

Rossing, Barbara R. *The Choice between Two Cities: Whore, Bride, and Empire in the Apocalypse.* HTS, 48. Harrisburg, PA: Trinity Press International, 1999.

———. *The Rapture Exposed: The Message of Hope in the Book of Revelation.* Boulder, CO: Westview, 2004.

Rotz, C. J., and J. A. du Rand. "The One Who Sits on the Throne: Towards a Theory of Theocentric Characterisation according to the Apocalypse of John." *Neot* 33 (1999) 91–111.

Rowland, Christopher. *The Open Heaven: A Study of Apocalyptic in Judaism and Early Christianity.* New York: Crossroad, 1982.

Rowley, H. H. *The Relevance of Apocalyptic: A Study of Jewish and Christian Apocalypses from Daniel to the Revelation.* New York: Association, 1963.

Royalty, R. M. *The Streets of Heaven: The Ideology of Wealth in the Apocalypse of John.* Macon, GA: Mercer University Press, 1998.

Ryrie, Charles C. *Dispensationalism.* Chicago: Moody, 1995.

Sals, U. *Die Biographie der "Hure Babylon": Studien zur Intertextualität der Babylon-Texte in der Bibel.* FAT, 2/6. Tübingen: Mohr Siebeck, 2004.

Sänger, D., ed. *Das Ezechielbuch in der Johannesoffenbarung*. Biblisch-Theologische Studien, 76. Neukirchen-Vluyn: Neukirchener, 2004.

Scherrer, Steven J. "Signs and Wonders in the Imperial Cult: New Look at a Roman Religious Institution in the Light of Rev 13:13–15." *JBL* 103 (1984) 599–610.

Schimanowski, G. *Die himmlische Liturgie in der Apokalypse des Johannes: Die frühjüdischen Traditionen in Offenbarung 4–5 unter Einschluss der Hekhalotliteratur*. WUNT 2/154. Tübingen: Mohr Siebeck, 2002.

Schmidt, D. D. "Semitisms and Septuagintalisms in the Book of Revelation." *NTS* 37 (1991) 592–603.

Scullard, Howard H. "Rome (History)." In *OCD*², 925–35.

Silberman, N. A. "Armageddon, Megiddo, and the End of the World." *Arch* 52 (1999) 36–37.

Slater, T. B. "On the Social Setting of the Revelation to John." *NTS* 44 (1998) 232–56.

Smith, C. R. "The Portrayal of the Church as the New Israel in the Names and Order of the Tribes in Revelation 7.5–8." *JSNT* 39 (1990) 111–18.

Smith, R. H. *Apocalypse: A Commentary on Revelation in Words and Images*. Collegeville: Liturgical, 2000.

Söding, Thomas. "Gott und das Lamm: Theozentrik und Christologie in der Johannesapokalypse." In *Theologie als Vision: Studien zur Johannes-Offenbarung*, edited by Knut Backhaus, 77–120. SBS, 191. Stuttgart: Katholisches Bibelwerk, 2001.

Spilsbury, P. *The Throne, the Lamb, and the Dragon: A Reader's Guide to the Book of Revelation*. Downers Grove, IL: InterVarsity, 2002.

Stefanovic, R. "The Angel at the Altar (Revelation 8:3–5): A Case Study on Intercalations in Revelation." *AUSS* 44 (2006) 79–94.

Stevenson, Gregory. *Temple and Identity in the Book of Revelation*. BZNW, 107. Berlin: de Gruyter, 2001.

Strabo. *Geography*. Translated by Horace Leonard Jones. 8 vols. Loeb Classical Library. Cambridge, MA: Harvard University Press, 1917–1932.

Stuckenbruck, L. T. *Angel Veneration and Christology: A Study in Early Judaism and in the Christology of the Apocalypse of John*. WUNT, 2/70. Tübingen: Mohr Siebeck, 1995.

Suetonius. Translated by J. C. Rolfe. 2 vols. Loeb Classical Library. Cambridge, MA: Harvard University Press, 1913–1914.

Suggit, J. N. *Oecumenius: Commentary on the Apocalypse*. FC, 112. Washington, D.C.: Catholic University of America Press, 2006.

Sutherland, C. H. V. *The Romans in Spain 217 B.C.–A.D. 117*. London: Methuen, 1939.

Swete, Henry B. *The Apocalypse of St. John: The Greek Text*. London: Macmillan, 1909.

Tacitus. *Agricola, Germania, Dialogus, the Histories, and the Annals*. Translated by C. H. Moore, et al. 5 vols. Loeb Classical Library. Cambridge, MA: Harvard University Press, 1914–1937.

Tavo, Felise. "The Ecclesial Notions of the Apocalypse in Recent Studies." *Currents in Biblical Research* 1 (2002) 112–36.

———. "The Outer Court and Holy City in Rev 11:1–2: Arguing for a Positive Appraisal." *ABR* 54 (2006) 56–72.

———. "The Structure of the Apocalypse: Re-Examining a Perennial Problem." *NovT* 47 (2005) 47–68.

Tenney, Merrill C. *Interpreting Revelation*. Grand Rapids: Eerdmans, 1957.

Thompson, Leonard L. *The Book of Revelation: Apocalypse and Empire*. New York: Oxford University Press, 1990.

Thompson, Steven. *The Apocalypse and Semitic Syntax*. SNTSMS, 52. Cambridge: Cambridge University Press, 1985.

Tóth, F. *Der himmlische Kult: Wirklichkeitskonstruktion und Sinnbildung in der Johannesoffenbarung*. Arbeiten zur Bibel und ihrer Geschichte, 22. Leipzig: Evangelische Verlagsanhalt, 2006.

Trebilco, Paul. *The Early Christians in Ephesus from Paul to Ignatius*. WUNT, 166. Tübingen: Mohr Siebeck, 2004.

Tucker, T. G. *Life in the Roman World of Nero and St. Paul*. New York: Macmillan, 1924.

Turner, W. L. *Making Sense of the Revelation: A Clear Message of Hope*. Macon, GA: Smyth and Helwys, 2000.

Van Kampen, Robert. *The Rapture Question Answered: Plain and Simple*. Grand Rapids: Baker, 1997.

VanderKam, James C., and William Adler, eds. *The Jewish Apocalyptic Heritage in Early Christianity*. CRINT, 3. Assen: Van Gorcum, 1996.

Waddell, Robby. *The Spirit of the Book of Revelation*. Journal of Pentecostal Theology: Supplement Series, 30. Blandford Forum, UK: Deo, 2006.

Wainwright, Arthur W. *Mysterious Apocalypse: Interpreting the Book of Revelation*. Nashville: Abingdon, 1993.

Walhout, Edwin. *Revelation Down to Earth: Making Sense of the Apocalypse of John*. Grand Rapids: Eerdmans, 2000.

Walvoord, John F. *The Blessed Hope and the Tribulation: A Biblical and Historical Study of Posttribulationism.* Grand Rapids: Zondervan, 1976.

———. *The Rapture Question: A Comprehensive Biblical Study of the Translation of the Church.* Grand Rapids: Zondervan, 1957.

———. *The Revelation of Jesus Christ: A Commentary.* Chicago: Moody, 1966.

Wenig, L. J. *The Challenge of the Apocalypse: Embracing the Book of Revelation with Hope and Faith.* New York: Paulist, 2002.

Wojciechowski, M. "Church as Israel according to the Revelation of St. John." *ColT* 64 (1994) special fascicle: 33–40.

Worth, R. H. *The Seven Cities of the Apocalypse and Greco-Asian Culture.* New York: Paulist, 1999.

———. *The Seven Cities of the Apocalypse and Roman Culture.* New York: Paulist, 1999.

Yamauchi, Edwin M. *The Archaeology of New Testament Cities in Western Asia Minor.* Baker Studies in Biblical Archaeology. Grand Rapids: Baker, 1980.

Yarbro Collins, Adela. "Satan's Throne. Revelations from Revelation." *BAR* 32 (2006) 26–39.

Zimmermann, R. "Die Virginitäts-Metapher in Apk 14:4–5 im Horizont von Befleckung, Loskauf und Erstlingsfrucht." *NovT* 45 (2003) 45–70.

Scripture Index

Note: A footnote is indicated by "n" at the appropriate page number. Hence "76n22" directs the reader to find the reference in footnote 22 on p. 76. When a reference is found both in the main text and in a footnote on the same page, text and note are separated by "/." Thus "87/n4" means the reference is to be found both in the main text on p. 87 and in footnote 4 on the same page.

Genesis

1	55
1:26–31	50
2:3	57
3:1–15	48
3:15	87
4:1	87/n4
4:25–26	87
5:29	87
9:26	87
12:1–3	87
13:13	54
13:14–17	87
15:13–20	87
18:25	87
23	87
29:31—30:24	76
35:22–26	76
37:9–10	47, 56
41:32	33, 54
46:8–27	76
49:2–27	76
49:9–10	53
49:10	87

Exodus

1–24	57
1:2–5	76
1:10	54
1:12	54
3:2	73
3:6	73
3:14	67
7–12	53, 57
7:14–24	49
9:7	76
9:8–12	49
9:22–35	49
9:26	76
10:12–20	49
10:21–29	49
12:13	76
14	57
15	58

Exodus - continued

15:17–18	87
16–19	58
19:4	48
19:5–6	98
19:6	56, 75
25:9	58
25:10–22	
25:40	58
26:30	58
27:1–8	58
28:17–21	79
30:1–10	58
30:17–21	58
31:11	58

Numbers

1–4	58
1:5–15	76
1:20–43	76
1:47–54	76n22
2:1–31	76
8:4	58
24:17–24	87
25:1–3	64
26	58
31:16	64
35:30	54

Deuteronomy

4:34	98
7:19	98
10:8–9	76n22
17:6	54
19:15	54
29:3	98

Joshua

5:14	73
6:2	73
13–19	76
14:3–5	76n22
21:43–45	88

Judges

5:19	94n11

2 Samuel

7	88

1 Kings

6:20	56, 79
7:23–26	58
12:29	76n22
16:31	64
17:1	53
21:25–26	64

2 Kings

6:17	110
23:29	94n11
25:27–29	88

1 Chronicles

28:5	63, 88
29:20	63, 88
29:23	63, 88

2 Chronicles

3:8	79
9:8	63
35:22	94n11

Job

26:12	48
41	48

Psalms

Book of	5n15
2:7–9	63
2:9	71
7:6–8	89
18:43–50	88
45:2–7	63
48:2	94n11
72	63, 88
74:13–14	48 [twice]
78:65–72	88
89:10	48
90:4	105, 117
104:26	48
110	63
118:10–14	94

Isaiah

Book of	5/n15, 6
2:1–4	89
4:2	53
6:2–3	58, 69
7:14–16	63, 88
8:1–8	88
8:8	63
9:1–7	63, 88
9:7	89n5
11	88
11:1	53, 71
11:2	55, 74
11:4	71
13–14	47, 58
13:10	58, 63
14:13	94n11
21:9	58
24–27	89
26:19	89
27:1	48
28:21	120
30:7	48
34:4	58, 63
47	58
51:9–10	48
53:2	53
53:7	53
59:20–21	97
60	59
65:17—66:24	89
65:17–25	59, 89n5

Jeremiah

5:14	53, 96
23:5–6	89
23:29	96
25:11–12	88
25:15–38	89
29:10	88
33:14–26	89

Ezekiel

Book of	5/n15
1	59
1:4	73
1:5–21	69
1:27–28	73
3:1–3	59
9	59
10	69
18:23	120
18:32	120
33:11	120
37–48	89
37	59
38–39	59, 89, 94, 105/n30
38:22	109
40–48	59
40–44	59, 63
43:7	59, 89, 89n5
43:10–11	63
47:1–12	59

Daniel

Book of	5, 6, 46
2	88
2:34–35	88
2:44–45	88
3	59
7	88
7:1–14	89
7:1–8	50, 80
7:1–7	59
7:7	48, 59
7:9–14	71, 88
7:9–13	59
7:9–12	89
7:9	72
7:14	89/n5
7:20	48, 59
7:21	93
7:24	48, 59
7:25	55, 60, 93
8:10	93
8:12	93
8:13	93, 94
8:14	55, 60, 93
8:24–25	93
9:1–19	88
9:20–27	88 [twice]
9:26	93
9:27	55, 60, 88, 93, 94, 97n17
10:5–6	73
11:21–39	63
11:25	93

11:31	94 [twice]	3:8	88
11:36–37	80	4	60
11:40—12:3	89	4:2	55, 74
11:40ff.	63	4:6	55, 74
12:1	60	4:10	74
12:2	89	4:10b	55
12:7	93	4:11–14	51, 53, 54
12:11	55, 60, 93, 94	6:1–8	60
12:12	93	6:9–14	88
		12:1–9	89
		12:1–6	94
		12:10—13:9	97
		14	60, 89
		14:1–15	94
		14:1–5	89

Hosea

6:5	96

Joel

1–2	63
2:4–11	63
2:4	60
3	89
3:1–16	60, 63, 89, 94
3:13	60/n27

Micah

4:1–8	89/n5

Haggai

2:20–23	88

Zechariah

Book of	5/n15
1:7–17	60
3–4	51

Malachi

Book of	6

Matthew

12:28	89
13:40–42	90
13:41–43	101
13:41	90
13:43	90
13:45–46	79
24	90
24:4–14	90
24:15–28	90
24:15	90, 94
24:23–24	81
24:29	90, 99
24:30–31	90

Matthew - continued

24:31	96
24:36	95
24:40–41	96
24:45–51	90
24:50	95
25:31–46	90, 108n37
25:31	90
25:46	90
28:19	78

Mark

1:15	89
3:27	102
8:29	89
8:34	78
8:38	95
13	90
13:1–23	63
13:5–13	90
13:14–23	90, 92
13:14	90, 94
13:24–27	63
13:24–25	90
13:24	99
13:26–27	90
13:27	96
13:30	63

Luke

11:20	89
17:34–35	96
19:11	89
21	90
21:8–19	90
21:20–25	90
21:20–24	90
21:25–26	49, 90
21:27	90
21:34–36	90
23:34	120
24:21	89

John

Book of	81
1:1	72
1:33	74
5:17–29	71
5:24–25	102
5:28–29	91, 108n37
6:15	89
6:39	91
6:40	91
6:44	91
6:54	91
11:24	91
12:48	91
14:1	91
14:2–3	91
14:25	74
14:26	74
15:18—16:4	91
15:26	74
16:1	113
16:4	113
16:33	77, 91

17:24	91	11:30–31	65
18:36–37	70	15	101
19:11	70	15:23	91
20:22	74	15:26	101
21:24	8	15:51–52	91
		15:54–55	101

Acts

1:6	89
1:11	89
3:21	89
7:60	120
15:15–19	75
16:14	16
19:1–10	13
19:23–41	15
24:15	108n37

Romans

2:4–5	119
2:5–16	91
2:29	76
8:19–23	101
8:23	51, 78
11:17–24	76
14:17	89

1 Corinthians

3:16	77
7:26–31	90
7:26	94
7:29	94
10:1–22	17

2 Corinthians

1:8	91
5:1	91

Galatians

6:16	76

Ephesians

2:11—3:6	76

Philippians

3:3	76
3:21	91, 101 [twice]
1:19–26	91

Colossians

1:13	89
2:1	13
2:8–19	13
2:11	76
4:12–16	13

1 Thessalonians

1:9	69
4:13–18	91
4:14	95
4:15	91, 99
4:17	96, 99

2 Thessalonians

1:6–10	91
1:7	95
1:8–9	101
2:1	99
2:3–12	91, 92
2:4	90
2:7	94
2:8	95, 99
2:9–12	81

1 Timothy

1:3–4	13
1:19–20	13
4:1–3	13
6:20	13

2 Timothy

4:6	91
4:16	120

Hebrews

12:28	89
13:10	76
13:13–15	76

James

1:18	51, 78
5:9	61

1 Peter

1:1	14
2:5	77
2:9–10	76, 98
2:9	56
4:1–4	14
5:8–10	14
5:8	103

2 Peter

3:8	105, 117

1 John

2:18	65, 93, 94
2:22	93
4:2	74
4:3	93

2 John

7	93

Revelation

1–3	31 [twice], 33, 44 [twice]
1	60
1:1–11	29, 30
1:1–3	2, 29, 30 [twice]

Scripture Index

1:1–2	3
1:1	4, 7, 8, 11, 30 [thrice], 33, 47, 62, 73
1:2	75
1:3	4, 5, 7, 11, 25, 27 [twice], 30 [twice], 62, 75
1:4–9	8
1:4–8	25
1:4–6	30
1:4–5	30
1:4–5a	29
1:4	7, 30, 55, 67, 74 [twice]/n16, 99, 112
1:5–6	104
1:5	25, 70 [twice], 71, 75, 82, 113
1:5b–6	29
1:6	26, 51, 56, 75, 98, 114
1:7–8	29, 30
1:7	30, 71 [twice]
1:8	30, 67, 68 [twice], 72
1:9—22:9	30
1:9–20	68
1:9–11	29, 30 [twice]
1:9	7, 11 [twice], 26, 61, 70, 71, 75 [twice], 92 [twice], 93, 94, 99, 104
1:10–16	73
1:10	3, 31 [thrice], 46, 73, 74
1:11	3, 9, 13, 30, 68
1:12–20	24, 32, 33
1:12–16	47
1:13–16	73
1:13	71
1:14	72
1:16	26, 71
1:17–18	113
1:17	72
1:18	70 [thrice], 80
1:19	3, 31, 50n11, 61
1:20	26, 47, 50 [twice], 51, 77
2–3	13, 26, 32 [twice], 33, 41, 55, 62n28, 68
2:1–17	42
2:1	3 [twice], 9, 32
2:2–3	83
2:2	27, 32
2:3	32
2:4–5	118
2:4	83
2:5	27, 83 [twice], 109
2:6	17 [twice], 27, 83 [twice]
2:7	3, 27 [twice], 32, 73, 74, 82, 118
2:8–11	94
2:8	3 [twice], 9, 32, 70 [twice], 72
2:9	11, 21/n47, 93
2:10–11	109, 118

Revelation - continued

2:10   11, 22, 34, 56, 61, 65 [twice], 83 [twice], 84, 93, 107, 118
2:11   3, 27 [twice], 32, 73, 74, 82
2:12   3 [twice], 9, 32 [twice]
2:13   11, 18, 22, 65, 70, 75, 83, 84 [twice], 93, 100
2:14–16   83
2:14–15   17
2:14   64, 76n22
2:16   17, 32, 61, 65, 71, 83, 109, 118
2:17   3, 27 [twice], 32, 73, 74, 82, 118
2:18—3:22   42
2:18–19   15
2:18   3 [twice], 9, 32, 72
2:19   27, 32, 83 [twice], 84
2:20–23   83
2:20   17, 64, 76n22
2:21–22   83
2:22   27, 32, 61, 65 [twice], 83
2:23   17, 27, 65, 83
2:25   83, 109, 118
2:26–28   32, 83, 109, 118
2:26   27 [thrice], 82, 83
2:27   71
2:28–29   33
2:29   3, 27, 73, 74
3:1–6   16
3:1   3 [twice], 9, 27, 32, 72, 74 [thrice], 83
3:2–3   118
3:2   27, 83
3:3   27 [twice], 61, 83, 95, 109
3:4–5   27, 51
3:4   32, 83
3:5–6   33
3:5   27, 32, 82, 118
3:6   3, 27, 73, 74
3:7   3 [twice], 9, 32, 71
3:8–11   34
3:8   27 [twice], 83
3:9   21/n47, 75, 93
3:10–11   61
3:10   27, 32 [twice], 83, 98
3:11   83, 118
3:12–13   33
3:12   27, 33, 53, 77, 82, 94, 118
3:13   3, 27, 73, 74
3:14   3 [twice], 9, 32, 70, 75
3:15   27, 83
3:18   27, 32, 51, 83, 118
3:20   27, 61, 109
3:21–22   33

Scripture Index

3:21   27, 33, 71, 72, 82, 104, 107, 109, 118
3:22   3, 27, 73, 74
4–22   31 [twice], 32, 33, 44 [twice], 62n28
4–5   25, 32, 61, 68 [twice], 71, 112
4:1–2   3, 31
4:1   31 [twice], 98
4:2   31, 59, 68, 73, 74
4:3   68, 69, 80
4:4   51, 56, 69
4:5   34, 50, 51, 74 [four times]
4:6–9   59, 69
4:6–7   41
4:6   58
4:7   55, 69
4:8–11   68
4:8   58, 67, 68 [twice]
4:9   68, 69
4:10   56, 68, 69 [twice], 114
4:11   70
5–22   68
5–8   68
5   40, 43, 59, 70
5:1–8   32
5:1–7   71, 113
5:1–5   25
5:1   72
5:5   69, 76n22
5:5–6   53
5:5   27, 46, 69, 71, 82
5:6–14   104, 113
5:6–7   109
5:6   50, 51, 55 [twice], 70, 71 [twice], 72 [twice], 74 [four times], 80, 80
5:7   69
5:8–14   26, 69 [thrice], 114
5:8   50, 51, 58 [twice]
5:9–10   70, 98
5:9   70 [twice], 71, 78, 82 [twice], 113, 117
5:10   75, 114
5:11–12   69
5:12   25, 70 [twice], 71, 118
5:13–14   70
5:13   69, 72
6–22   29, 31n3, 32, 34 [twice]/n5, 36, 38, 39, 40, 41 [twice], 42 [twice], 44, 91, 100
6:1—15:4   42
6–14   43
6   25, 26, 28, 34, 36, 40, 61
6:1–8   3, 41, 43, 60, 92
6:2   41n12
6:9–11   22, 26, 38, 41, 43, 77, 83, 92, 93, 100, 104, 107, 120

Revelation - continued

6:9	58, 70, 75, 108
6:10	120
6:11	27, 32, 44, 51
6:12–17	41, 42, 43, 58, 61
6:12–14	92
6:15–17	38, 77, 92, 101
6:16–17	72, 119
6:16	69
7	29n2, 38 [twice], 39, 40, 61, 77
7:1–8	26, 38, 43, 77
7:1–4	59
7:1–3	98
7:1–2	55
7:2	32, 69
7:3	76
7:4–8	58, 76
7:4	56 [twice]
7:5–8	56, 76
7:5	76n22
7:6	76n22
7:7	76n22
7:8	76n22
7:9–17	38, 77
7:9–14	26
7:9–10	71, 72
7:9	27, 32, 51
7:10	69
7:13–14	3, 50, 51 [twice]
7:13	27, 32, 69
7:14–17	107
7:14	11, 32, 42, 53, 61, 65, 70, 77, 82, 92, 93, 117
7:15–17	26, 38, 43 [thrice], 61, 119
7:15	51, 53, 69, 77, 94, 98, 114
7:17	71, 72
8–9	28 [twice], 49 [twice], 57, 61, 119
8:1–5	25, 34, 36, 42, 92, 101
8:1	29, 37, 40, 41
8:2	37, 40, 74n17
8:3–5	34n5, 37, 40, 41, 58 [twice]
8:3–4	69
8:3	69
8:6—21:8	39
8:5	29, 34, 43
8:6—9:21	34, 36, 40
8:8–13	92
8:6–12	41
8:7–12	43
8:13	39n11, 41
9	10, 43
9:1–19	92
9:1–11	49
9:1–2	105
9:1	42, 50
9:4	32, 38, 43, 76, 98
9:7–11	60
9:7	60

9:9	94, 95	11:3–4	50, 51, 54
9:12	42	11:3	39, 70, 75, 93
9:13	42, 58	11:4–13	26, 39
9:16–19	60	11:4	50, 53, 60
9:16–17	94, 95	11:5–6	53, 96
9:16	9	11:6	75
9:20–21	26, 83 [twice], 120	11:7–10	54, 83, 98
9:20	27, 76n22	11:7	22, 25, 60, 70, 75, 80, 93, 105
9:21	17	11:8	47 [twice], 53, 70
10:1—11:13	38, 39	11:10	54, 75 [twice]
10–11	68	11:11–13	43
10	3, 37, 38, 39n10, 40, 43	11:11–12	98
10:1–3	73 [twice]	11:14–19	34, 36, 39, 40
10:1	73	11:14	42
10:4	3	11:15–19	37, 42, 43, 61, 68, 101, 119
10:5–7	6, 38	11:15–18	72, 92
10:6	69	11:15	42, 71 [twice], 92
10:7	75, 86	11:17	67, 68
10:8–11	38, 59	11:18	43, 68, 75, 92 [twice], 108n37, 118 [twice], 119
10:11—11:1	39n10		
10:11	5, 43, 75	11:19	34, 58 [twice], 92
11	61 [thrice]	12–15	39/n10, 41, 68
11:1–13	37, 38, 39n10, 40	12:1—15:4	99
11:1–3	53	12–14	104n29
11:1–2	3, 59, 77/n25	12:1—14:5	35, 36 [thrice], 40
11:1	58, 77	12–13	35, 61
11:2–3	55, 60	12	35, 48n7 [thrice], 61
11:2	39, 77, 93	12:1–6	98
11:3–12	118	12:1–5	63
11:3–7	75	12:1–2	36, 47
11:3–6	53		

Revelation - continued

12:1	35, 56
12:3–17	36
12:3–4	47
12:3	9, 48, 48, 54, 80
12:4–12	80
12:4–6	47, 77
12:4	48
12:5–6	94
12:5	69, 71 [twice], 104, 109
12:6—14:5	92
12:6–17	63
12:6	35, 55, 60, 93
12:7–12	104, 107
12:7–9	60, 113
12:7	35
12:9	48, 52, 80
12:10–11	113
12:10	71, 72, 109
12:11	27, 70 [twice], 75, 82 [twice], 96
12:12	56, 93, 109, 113
12:12a	107
12:13–17	98
12:13–16	48, 58, 77
12:13	93
12:14	35, 55, 60, 93
12:15–16	58
12:16	58n22
12:17—13:5	48
12:17—13:1	80
12:17	26, 27, 35, 48, 70, 75, 77, 83, 93, 118
13	36, 52, 93, 96, 105, 114
13:1–10	25, 35
13:1	9, 19, 54, 59, 61, 80 [twice], 105
13:2	50, 59, 80
13:3–4	77
13:3	52, 80
13:4	24, 35, 78, 80 [twice]
13:5–7	59
13:5–6	61, 80
13:5	19, 35, 55, 60, 93
13:7–8	24, 81
13:7	22, 35, 60, 77, 80, 83, 93
13:8	70, 77, 82, 114
13:9	27
13:10–11	26
13:10	22, 32, 77, 80, 83 [twice], 84, 93, 118
13:11–18	25, 35
13:11	81
13:12–17	62
13:12–15	49
13:12	77, 78, 81
13:13–15	81
13:13	20
13:14–15	59, 80
13:14	19, 81
13:15	19, 93, 100
13:16–18	81
13:16–17	20, 22

Scripture Index 153

13:16	93
13:18	49, 55
14	39, 61 [twice]
14:1–5	35, 36, 38 77, 107
14:1	56 [twice], 78
14:2–3	26
14:3–4	50, 51
14:3	56 [twice], 69, 78
14:4–5	26, 78n26, 118
14:4	78 [twice]/n26, 82, 83, 117
14:5	78, 81
14:6—19:21	25
14:6–13	38, 39, 40 [twice]
14:6–11	39n11, 43
14:6–7	39, 40
14:8	39, 40, 58, 78/n26, 81
14:9–11	39, 40, 83
14:10–11	120
14:10	119
14:11–13	118
14:11	81
14:12–13	39, 40, 80
14:12	26, 27, 32, 83 [twice], 84
14:13	3, 4, 22, 26, 27, 73, 74, 83, 107, 117
14:14—15:4	35, 36, 39, 42
14:14–20	40, 43, 60, 61, 92, 94, 101
14:14–16	35, 60n27, 72
14:14	59, 71 [twice]
14:15	58 [twice]
14:17–20	35
14:17–18	58
14:17	58
14:18	58
14:20	56, 95
15–20	44
15–16	61
15:1	37 [twice], 40, 43, 47, 48
15:2–4	26, 35, 37, 40, 43, 58, 107, 118
15:2	27, 36, 58, 82, 83
15:3–4	26, 68
15:3	68 [twice]
15:5—22:9	42 [twice]
15:5—16:21	34, 36, 40 [twice]
15:5—16:12	92
15:5–8	58 [twice]
15:6	51
15:7	69
16	28, 42, 49 [twice], 57, 119
16:1	58
16:2–10	43
16:2	32, 43, 49
16:3–4	49
16:4–6	43
16:5–7	42, 68

Revelation - continued

16:5	67
16:6	22, 75, 83, 93, 100
16:7	58, 68
16:9	83, 120
16:10	32, 43, 49, 120
16:11	27, 83
16:12–16	94, 105
16:13–17	26
16:13–16	60, 92
16:13–14	50, 52, 81, 103n26
16:13	25, 35, 55, 81
16:14	44, 68, 95
16:15	4, 27, 32, 95, 101
16:16	38, 94, 95
16:17–21	42, 43, 61, 92, 101
16:17	43, 58, 69
16:18	34
16:19	38, 119
16:20	43
16:21	17, 49
17:1—19:10	31n3 [twice], 34, 35 [twice], 36, 38, 40 [twice]
17–18	61, 114
17	52, 61 [thrice]
17:1–3	3
17:1	34 [twice]
17:2	34, 81
17:3–13	92
17:3–6	25
17:3	3, 34, 59, 73, 74, 80 [twice]
17:4	62
17:5	34, 47 [twice], 78
17:6	22, 47, 70, 83, 93 [twice], 100
17:7–18	3, 51
17:7	59, 80
17:8–14	25
17:8	80, 82, 105, 114
17:9–12	50
17:9	9, 49, 51
17:9–10	61, 80
17:10–11	8n24, 35, 50
17:10	51, 56, 93
17:11	52/n13
17:12–14	52, 59
17:12–13	55
17:12	81
17:14	25, 26, 43 [twice], 71, 82, 84, 92, 94, 101
17:15—19:5	92
17:15–18	25
17:15	50, 52
17:16–17	43 [twice], 120
17:18	9, 47, 50, 52, 54, 62, 81
18	25, 52n14 [twice]
18:2ff.	58
18:3	78, 81
18:4	16, 26
18:6	27, 83
18:7	47
18:9	26, 81

18:11–17	61	19:11–21	60, 94, 96, 102, 107, 109
18:12–13	15	19:11–16	36, 105
18:20	26, 43, 75, 107	19:11	35 [twice], 41n12, 95, 102n26
18:24	75, 83, 93 [twice], 100	19:12	72
19	102	19:13	72, 96
19–20	39/n10, 41, 68, 104n29	19:14–15	95
19:1–10	25, 42	19:14	27, 32, 51, 96
19:1–9	43, 119	19:15	32, 61, 65, 68, 71 [twice], 82, 96, 119
19:1–8	26, 101	19:16	25, 71
19:1–4	68	19:17–21	36, 38, 59, 105
19:2	22, 43, 83, 93, 100, 120	19:17	102n26, 105n30
19:4	69	19:18–19	81
19:5	69	19:18	101
19:6–8	92	19:19–21	35, 100
19:6	68 [twice]	19:19	35, 95, 102n26, 105
19:7–9	26, 38, 118	19:20–21	71
19:7–8	78/n26, 114	19:20	35, 81, 96, 102n26, 103n26 [twice], 120
19:8	26, 50, 51, 96		
19:9–11	3		
19:9	3 [twice], 4, 31n3, 35, 36	19:21	32, 61, 65, 71, 82, 95 [thrice] 96, 101, 105n30
19:10–21	92		
19:10	3, 31n3, 35, 70, 73 [twice], 75	20–22	33 [twice]
19:11—21:8	31n3, 35, 36 [twice], 36, 40 [twice], 99, 102n26, 104	20	61, 99, 102, 116
		20:1–10	35, 36, 102n26, 104 [twice]
		20:1–6	89n5, 110
19:11—20:10	110	20:1–3	100, 101, 102, 113
19:11—20:4	95, 96	20:1	50, 102n26

Revelation - continued

20:2–7	57
20:2	48
20:3	35, 52, 56 [twice], 93 [twice], 102n26
20:4–6	25, 43, 59, 92, 100, 101, 108n37, 109, 119
20:4–5	105
20:4	22, 27, 52 [twice], 70, 75 [twice], 83, 93, 96, 102/n26, 103n26, 107 [twice], 108n35
20:5	50, 52, 101, 105, 109n37
20:6	4, 26, 27, 38, 51, 52, 21, 105, 108, 114
20:7–10	59, 60, 92, 94, 100, 101, 110
20:7–9	93, 104
20:7–9a	107
20:7	95, 105
20:8–9	105n30
20:8–9a	105
20:8	35, 55
20:9	58, 109 [thrice]
20:9b–10	105 [twice]
20:10—21:8	72
20:10	81, 103n26, 120
20:11—21:8	100
20:11–15	36, 105
20:11–14	92
20:11	69, 102n26
20:12–15	108n37
20:12–13	83
20:12	27, 101, 102n26
20:13	27, 83, 92
20:14	52, 61, 108, 109n37 [twice]
20:15	101, 120
21–22	61, 104n29
21	59, 61 [twice]
21:1–8	36 [twice], 42, 43, 92, 105, 119
21:1	102n26, 108
21:2	36, 38, 78n26, 102n26, 114
21:3–8	68
21:3–4	38
21:3	53, 77
21:5	3 [twice], 31n3, 36, 69
21:6	68, 72
21:7	27, 82
21:8	17, 27, 76n22, 83
21:9—22:9	31/n3, 34, 35 [twice], 36, 40 [twice], 44, 78
21:9—22:5	43, 89n5, 92, 114, 119 [twice]
21:9ff.	38
21:9–10	3, 25, 54
21:9	34 [thrice], 78/n26, 114
21:10—22:5	59

21:10	3, 34 [twice], 35, 73, 74, 79	22:7	4, 5, 7, 27, 30 [twice], 75
21:11–22	25, 78, 79	22:8–11	3
21:11	79	22:8–9	35, 73 [twice]
21:12–14	98	22:8	7, 73
21:12–13	79	22:8b–9	30, 31n3
21:12	56	22:9	27, 75
21:14	56, 79	22:10–21	30
21:15–18	79	22:10–15	27
21:15–17	59	22:10–11	30
21:15	3	22:10	5, 30 [twice], 75
21:16–17	38	22:12–13	30
21:16	56	22:12	27, 30 [twice], 83, 118
21:17	56, 84	22:13	30, 72 [twice]
21:19–20	56, 79	22:14–16	30
21:21	79	22:14–15	84
21:22—22:5	60	22:14	4, 30
21:22	53, 59, 68 [twice], 77, 79, 94	22:15	17, 76n22, 81, 83
21:23—22:5	25, 78, 79	22:16	3, 30, 71, 75
21:23	79	22:17–20	30
21:24–26	79	22:17	73, 74
21:27	17, 27, 79, 81	22:18–19	3
22:1–5	42	22:18	5, 27, 75
22:1–2	59, 79	22:19	5, 19, 75
22:1	3, 69, 72	22:20	3, 30 [twice]
22:3	69, 72, 79	22:21	8, 30 [twice]
22:3b–4	79		
22:5	79		
22:6–21	29, 68		
22:6–9	31		
22:6	3 [twice], 30 [twice], 31n3, 35, 36, 75		
22:6b–8a	30		

Subject Index

Alpha and Omega
    Referring to God, 68
    Referring to Christ, 72
Amillennialism: See Non-
    chiliasm.
Antagonists, trio of, 37n8,
    52, 55, 79–82
Antichrist, 93
    See also: Beast.
Antiochus Epiphanes IV,
    6, 55, 63, 94
Antipas, 11–12, 22,
    64–65, 117
"Apocalypse," 4, 24
Apocalyptic literature,
    3, 6
    Contrasted with
        prophecy, 6–7/
        nn17–19
Armageddon, 94, 101,
    102
    Concept applied
        to John's
        circumstances, 32,
        65, 94–96, 104–7
    Final 109, 110
Asia Minor, 3, 7, 9,
    13–27, 65, 67, 70,
    83, 85, 95, 104,
    110, 111, 112, 113,
    116–117
    Urban centers of, 13
    Cradle of 2nd cent.
        Christianity, 14
    Economic prosperity,
        15
    Romanized, 23–24
Audience: See Recipients.
Augustus, 14, 15, 18
Author, 7–8/nn20–23
Babylon, 34–35, 47,
    81–82, 117
"Balaam," 64
Beast, 9, 10, 12, 25, 35,
    80, 93, 114
    Mark of the, 20, 22,
        49–50, 81
    Seven heads of the, 50,
        51–52, 54
    Ten horns of the, 52,
        54, 55
Body of the book,
    divided into two
    complementary
    parts, 33, 41, 44
Bowl-plagues, 34–42, 43,
    48–49
Bowls, Golden (prayers of
    saints), 51

Subject Index

Bride of the Lamb, 25, 26, 34–35, 54, 78
Canonicity, 2–4, 10
Cavalry, 9, 95
Chain links: See Clasps, literary.
Chapter divisions, traditional, 29
Chiasm(us)
   In prescript/postscript, 30
   In introductory formulae of major sections, 31
   In combat material 35–36, 37
   In Rev 21, 78–79
Chiliasm, 101–2
Christ, 70–73, and passim
   Death and resurrection, 1, 70
   True king, 24, 71–72, 114
   Care of churches, 26
   Speaker of the seven oracles 32
   Faithful witness, 70, 117
   Executor of God's will, 71
   Messiah, 71
   Deity of, 72
   Angel-christology?, 73
   Victor now and in future, 113
China, 9
Christians
   Distinct from society, 1, 77–78, 112, 114
   Persecution of, 12, 21–22, 25–26, 54, 55, 77, 79, 92–94, 97–99, 111–12
Church, The, 47–48, 51, 53, 75–79
   Continuous with Israel, 75–76, 97–98
   Prophetic, 53, 74–75, 81
   Priestly, 26, 51, 53, 75, 78–79, 114
   Royal, 51, 53, 75, 78–79, 114
Churches, The seven of Asia, 8–9/n25
"City" (community), 79
Clasps, literary, 37–38/n9
Combat motif, 35–36, 93, 94–96, 100
Conical structure: See Recapitulation.
"Conquering," 27, 32–33, 82, 118, 121
Contrast, as a literary device
   Between ladies Jerusalem and Babylon, 34–35

Between two fundamental loyalties, 81–82, 114–16
Counterfeiting of the good by the evil, 79–82
Cyclical structure: See Recapitulation.
Creation, God's work of, 70, 114
Criticism, biblical, 2, 7–8, 62–63
Cubed numbers, numerological significance of, 56–57
Date of the Revelation, 8/n24
Dispensationalism, 1–2/n3, 11n29, 45, 89n5, 96–99
Domitian, emperor, 8, 9, 50, 85, 117, 111
  Reign of terror, 17
  Honored at Ephesus, 18
  Accepted divine honors, 19
  Persecutor of church?, 22/n48
Doubling of revelation, 33

Diplopia in the millennial vision, 104–5/n29
Dragon, 9, 35, 36, 45, 48, 52, 57–58, 61, 80, 93
  Seven heads of the, 54
  Ten horns of the, 54
  Binding of, for 1,000 years, 107, 110
"Egypt" (Roman society), 53–54
Elders, The twenty-four, 56, 69
End, Parallel depictions of the, 42–43
Endurance: See Perseverance.
Ephesus, 7, 9, 13–14, 15, 18, 20, 23, 112
Eschatology, 85–110 and passim
  Soteriological and ethical goal of, 85
  Rules for interpreting, 86
  OT scheme of, 86–89
  NT scheme of, 89–91
  Core of, in Rev, 91–92, 110
  Tribulation, 92–94
  Armageddon, 94–96
  Rapture?, 96–99
  Millennium?, 99–110
Ethics, 7, 25–27, 83, 111

European Common Market, 9
Exodus motif, 48–49, 57–58, 64, 76
Evil, 12, 112, 119, 121
Faith as a virtue, 84
Faithfulness, 84, 117–19
False prophet, 35, 37n8, 52, 55, 61, 81–82, 93, 101
Five
  Units, 33–34, 41–42
Foreshadowing, 38, 39, 40
Formula
  Concluding, 31n3, 34, 35, 36
  Interpreting ("A is B") 50–53, 107
"Fornication" (participation in godless society), 81
Four
  Units, 33, 40, 41–42
  Symbol of totality, 55
  Living creatures, 69
Frogs (demons), 52
Futurist school of interpretation, 10, 11n29, 28, 46, 61
God
  Sovereign, 1, 12, 25, 67–70, 112–13
  Overcomer of evil, 12, 112, 119, 121
  Worship of, in heaven, 24–25, 26, 68–70
  Revealer of the visions, 2–3, 12, 32
  "He who is etc.," 67–68
  "Alpha and Omega," 68
  Beginning and end, 68
  Almighty, 68
  Throne, 68–69
  "One who lives for ever," 69
  Good, 119–121
Harlot, 9, 12, 25, 34, 47, 52, 62, 81, 93, 114, 117
"Hearing," 27
Hero veneration: See Imperial cult.
Historicist school of interpretation, 10, 28, 46, 61
"Hour of trial," 32
Hundred forty-four thousand, The: See Numbers, 144,000.
Hymns, 26, 42, 58, 70
Hyperbole, 11, 62, 65, 103, 104–110, 116
Idealist school of interpretation, viii,

10–11/n29, 28, 46, 61, 65
Imitation
  of Lamb by his followers, 77–78, 83, 117
  of Lamb by beast, 80
Imminence, 62
Imperial cult, 18–22, 24, 25, 61–62, 70, 80, 112
Inclusio
  Seals/New Jerusalem, 38
  Trumpets/Combat Resolved, 39
  Alpha and Omega, 68
Inspiration, 2–3, 5
Interlocking: See Clasps, literary.
Interpretation
  Four main schools of, 10–11, 28, 46, 61
  of symbols: See Symbols.
  Rules of, in eschatology, 86
Jerusalem
  Symbol of people of God, 31n3, 34–3537n8, , 56, 78–79, 81–82
  Symbol of earthly city that crucifies Jesus and God's people, i.e. Rome, 53–54
Jesus: See Christ.
Jews as slanderers of Christians, 21/n47
Judgment, General, 39–40, 83, 89, 90, 91, 92, 99, 100, 108n37, 110
"Jezebel," 64, 65
"Keeping"
  Of believers keeping God's ways, 4, 27
  Of Christ keeping believers in time of trial, 98
Kingdom of God
  Invisibly realized since Jesus's first advent 71, 89, 104, 113
  Finally to be manifest on earth, 89/n5
Lamb, 45/n45, 53, 71
Lampstand (church), 47, 50, 51
Left Behind Series novels, 1–2/n2
Letter, stylized elements of, 8–9, 29–30
Letters, The seven to the churches: See Oracles, The seven.
Linear plot development, 28, 42–44

Linen, Fine (righteous deeds), 26, 51, 96, 118
Living creatures, The four, 69
Lion, 53
Locusts, 10, 49, 60, 63
Mark of the beast, 20, 22, 49–50, 81, 83
Martyrdom of Christians, 1, 11, 22, 25, 26, 52, 64–65, 83, 93, 97, 99, 100, 110, 117
Middle East, 9
Mid-tribulation rapture theory, 96–99
Millennium, 99–110
  Not equivalent to OT expectation of God's kingdom on earth, 89n5
  Figure of 1,000, 56–57, 105, 117
  Interpreted dynamically, 117
  See also: Dragon, Binding of, for 1,000 years; Resurrection, The first.
Moral breakdown, 16–17
"Mystery," 47
Nero, 17, 49n9
  Redivivus, 51–52/n13, 80/n29
New heaven and new earth, 119–121
Nicolaitans, 17, 64, 65
Non-chiliasm
  Augustinian-allegorical, 102–3
  Parabolic, 103
Numbers
  Numerology, 37n8, 54–57
  Particular numbers:
  2, 54
  3, 55
  3 1/2, 55
  4, 55
  6, 55
  7, 55
  10, 55
  12, 56
  24, 56
  144, 56
  666, 49–50, 81
  1000 years, 57, 105
  "1600 stadia," 56
  "12,000 stadia," 56
  144,000, 35, 38, 51, 56–57, 76–78, 81
Old Testament, John's use of, 5, 6, 57–60, and passim

Olivet discourse of Jesus, 90
Oracles, The Seven, to the churches, 31–33, 33–34
Papacy, Renaissance, as Antichrist, 10
Parousia (of Christ)
  image, applied to John's day, 61, 65, 96, 106–7, 109
  Final, 63, 90, 91, 92, 94–95, 96–99, 101, 102, 105, 109, 110
Pax Romana, 14–15
Pergamum, 9, 11, 13, 22, 32, 64
  Titular capital of Asia, 15/n15
  "Satan's throne"?, 18
Persecution of Christians, 12, 21–22, 25–26, 54, 55, 77, 79, 92–94, 97 99, 111–12
Perseverance, 12, 25–27, 96–99
Plagues, 119–120
  See also: Seals; Trumpet-plagues; Bowl-plagues
Postscript, 29–30, 31
Post-tribulation rapture theory, 96–97
Predestination, 82

Pre-millennialism: See Chiliasm.
Prescript, 2–12, 29–30, 30–31
Preterist Idealism, vii-viii, 11–12, 61–66
Preterist school of interpretation, viii, 10, 11n29, 28, 46, 62–63, 65, 95
Pre-tribulation rapture theory, 96–99
Pre-wrath rapture theory, 96
Prophecy, 5–7, 71–75, 86, 113–114
  As warfare, 65, 95–96, 105
Prophet, False: See False prophet.
Prosperity
  Roman, 14–16
  Modern First World, 111
Proximity of the ultimate, principle of 11, 63–64, 86–88, 92, 116–17
Punishment, everlasting, 120
Rapture?, 96–99
Reality, Alternative view of in prophecy, 24–25, 113–14

Recapitulation, 28–29, 42–44, 85, 91–92
Recipients, 8–10, 13–27
Redemption, theme of hymns, 70
Resurrection, General, 35, 89, 91, 99, 100, 108–9n37, 110
Resurrection, The "first," 52–53, 106, 107–8
Reversal of fortunes, for faithful Christians, 25, 100, 114
Reverse typology, Technique of: See Typology, Reverse.
Rewards, 1, 27, 83, 118
Riders, Four, on horses, 41/n12
Rome
   Imperial, 9, 13, 15, 16, 18, 22–23, 24, 25, 47, 50, 51, 54, 81–82, 112, 113, 114, 117
   Seven hills, 9/n27
Root of David, 53
Salvation
   Grounded on God's eternal purpose, 82
   Founded on Lamb's blood, 82
   Through perseverance, 27, 83–84, 118–19
Scrolls
   Large, of Rev 5, 32, 40, 70
   Small, of Rev 10, 38–39/n10, 40, 99
   Parallelism of the two, 43
Seals, 28–29, 34–42, 43
Seven, numerological significance of, 55
   spirits of God, 74
"Show," 4, 46
"Sign," "Signify," 4, 46–47, 47–50
Six, 55
Six hundred sixty-six, 49–50, 55
"Sodom" (Rome), 47, 53
Spirit, The, 73–75
   Seven spirits of God, 74
   of prophecy, 74–75
"Spiritual" interpretation of symbols, 47
Squared numbers, numerological significance of, 56
Stage machinery, in imperial cults, 19–20
Star (angel), 50
Structure, literary, 28–44
Symbol, 1, 4–5, 9, 45–66
   Definition, 45

Purpose, 4–5, 44, 45/n1
Simile, 46
Metaphor, 46
Temple
  Symbol for the church, 53, 77
Temporary earthly messianic kingdom, in Judaism, 106/n32
Ten, numerological significance of, 55
Three
  Units, 33, 40, 41–42
  Antagonists, 55
Three-and-a-half years, 55, 93–94
Torches, The seven (Spirit(s) of God), 51, 74
Trade associations, 16
Tribulation, 25–26, 32, 61, 65, 77, 92–94
Trumpet-plagues, 28, 34 and passim in pp. 34–42, 49
Twelve, numerological significance of, 55–56
Twenty-four elders: See Elders, The twenty-four.
Typology, 49, 64

Reverse, 64–66, 92, 104/n29, 104–7, 110, 116
Two
  Units, 33–34, 41–42
  Witnesses, 51, 53, 54
"Understanding," 49–50
Vengeance, 120–21
Ventriloquism, 19
Vials of God's wrath: See Bowl-plagues.
"Virginity" (abstention from godless society), 78
Visions of Rev 6–22
  Analyzed into seven, 34–41
  Subdivided into two scrolls 38–41
War motif: See Combat motif.
Washing robes, 53
Waters (peoples), 52
White garments, 27, 32
  see also: Linen, Fine.
Witnesses, The two, 51, 53, 54, 98
Woman (Rev 12), 47–48
"Works," 27, 83; cf. 118–19
Worship scenes, in heaven, 24–25, 26, 68–70
Whore, see Harlot.

"Wisdom," 49–50
Wrath of God, 38, 42, 43, 49, 72, 119

www.ingramcontent.com/pod-product-compliance
Lightning Source LLC
Chambersburg PA
CBHW050810160426
43192CB00010B/1711